Ken Hom's Asian Ingredients

photographs by
Susanne Kaspar

Ken Hom's
ASIAN INGREDIENTS

A GUIDE WITH RECIPES

by Ken Hom

TEN SPEED PRESS
BERKELEY, CALIFORNIA

A Kirsty Melville book

Ten Speed Press
P.O. Box 7123
Berkeley, CA 94707

Distributed in Australia by E.J. Dwyer Pty Ltd; in Canada by
Publishers Group West; in New Zealand by Tandem Press;
in South Africa by Real Books; and in the United Kingdom
and Europe by Airlift Books.

Text and cover design by Nancy Austin
Food styling by Sue White
Printed in Hong Kong

Library of Congress Cataloging in Publication Data
Hom, Ken.
    [Asian ingredients]
    Ken Hom's Asian ingredients / by Ken Hom.
          p. cm.
    Includes index.
    ISBN 0-89815-795-1
    1. Cookery, Oriental. 2. Cookery, Chinese. I. Title.
TX724.5.A1H596   1996
641.595—dc20   95–40846
                                    CIP

1 2 3 4 5 6 7 8 9 10 — 99 98 97 96

Contents

Introduction / vii

Equipment and Techniques / 1

Vegetables / 13

Ingredients / 47

Recipes / 103

Index / 143

Resources / 149

About the Author / 152

Introduction

Despite the number of Asian and Chinese cookery books published every year, many cooks still have a limited knowledge of Asian ingredients. Although more chefs and home cooks are working with Asian ingredients, much confusion about the ingredients has developed as these flavors have become increasingly popular. In response, I offer my informed and, I hope, unbiased advice to guide you through the Asian market. Here you'll find basic information on what to look for when shopping for these unfamiliar ingredients, how to use them, store them, and which brands to buy. Using the book's photos as a visual guide, you'll be sure to buy the same ingredients that Asian cooks everywhere use to produce savory and authentic dishes.

As you'll soon discover, with a little effort you can duplicate many of the culinary wonders of Asia. In China, Hong Kong, Taiwan, Australia, and Europe, as well as North America, there is a wide variety of readily available Asian food and ingredients. This, of course, is most true in the East, where the markets are full of seemingly exotic vegetables—wild rice shoots, fresh straw mushrooms, fresh bamboo shoots, smoked garlic, pea shoots, yellow cucumbers—in a variety that is impossible to find in the West. However, most ingredients, seasonings, and vegetables are now available in western markets as trade continues to expand and an international style of Asian cooking spreads. As a result, almost all the ingredients profiled in this book can be purchased in ordinary supermarkets or Asian or Chinese groceries and markets. In fact, in Asian and Chinese markets in almost every country, there may be dozens of varieties of chile bean pastes and sauces. Sometimes the different condiments available in the best Asian markets are too numerous to count.

This guide does not include all Asian ingredients and is not intended to be an encyclopedia—it is a quick-reference book that will enable you to better use your other cookbooks and to stock your pantry as I have stocked mine. I have, however, endeavored to include the most commonly used ingredients as well as those that arouse the most curiosity, such as bird's nest and shark's fin. In case the preferred ingredient cannot be found, I have listed substitutes that are acceptable, but you will almost always achieve the best results by using the one suggested. Whenever you're headed to the market for Asian ingredients, take this guide with you.

Surveying the basic ingredients I have included, you might think there is a limit to the number of dishes that could result from the various combinations, yet as I have witnessed again and again there are always new surprises. As you experiment with the essential Asian ingredients, you too will be amazed and delighted by the limitless possibilities.

Over the centuries, Asians have developed a unique culinary style, a special approach and philosophy concerning food. Two directives have defined and guided the world's Asian cuisines: use only the freshest ingredients and balance the flavors. Thus, you will notice that the Asian cooks use spices and flavorings but never overwhelmingly so. Ginger, scallions, garlic, Shaoxing rice wine, soy sauce, chile bean sauce, and other seasonings are distinctly but never obtrusively present. As you cook with the ingredients, be sure to observe these guidelines.

Whenever I travel to Chinatowns throughout the world or to Hong Kong, Bangkok, Kuala Lumpur, Jakarta, Taiwan, or China, whether in markets, restaurants, or private homes, I always encounter a variety of flavorful Asian foods presented in an atmosphere redolent of aromatic herbs, spices, and condiments. Despite regional variations, one senses a unity of style that comes from shared techniques, flavors, ingredients, and beliefs that are unique to Asian and especially Chinese cuisine.

Understanding the East's rich and varied culinary traditions begins with the knowledge of the essential ingredients. As you learn more about the components that create the distinctive taste of Asian cuisines, I hope you will be tempted to use the essential sauces, spices, vegetables, and other ingredients in your daily cooking. I share your excitement and wish you happy cooking!

EQUIPMENT & TECHNIQUES

Equipment

Although traditional Asian cooking equipment is not essential for the preparation of Asian food, there are some tools that will make it much easier. Moreover, as you will see below, there is a gain when one relies upon implements that have been use-tested over many centuries. You can purchase most of the items listed below at a fairly moderate price in gourmet shops, Chinese or Asian food shops, or supermarkets.

WOK

A most useful and versatile piece of equipment, the wok may be used for stir-frying, blanching, deep-frying, and steaming foods. Its deep sides and either tapered or slightly flattened but round bottom allow for quick, even, and fuel-efficient cooking. In stir-frying, the wok's deep sides prevent the food and oils from spilling over; in deep-frying, much less oil is required because of the concentration of heat and ingredients at the wok's base.

There are two basic types of wok: the traditional Cantonese version, with short rounded handles on either side of the edge or lip of the wok, and the *pau* wok, with one long handle from 12 to 14 inches (30 to 35 cm) long.

Choosing a Wok

For the best results, choose a wok that is 12 to 14 inches (30 to 35 cm) in diameter with deep sides. It is easier—and safer—to cook a small batch of food in a large wok than it is to cook a large quantity in a small one. Be aware that some modernized woks are shallow or flat-bottomed and thus no better than a frying pan. A heavier wok, preferably made of carbon steel, is superior to the lighter stainless steel or aluminum types, which cannot take very high heat and therefore tend to scorch themselves and food.

Seasoning a Wok

All woks (except nonstick ones) need to be seasoned. Many need to be scrubbed first to remove the machine oil that is applied to the surface by the manufacturer to protect it in transit. This is the *only* time you will ever scrub your wok—unless you let it rust up. Scrub it with a cream cleanser and water to remove as much of the machine oil as possible. Then dry it and put it on the stove. Using paper towels, rub 2 tablespoons (30 ml) of vegetable oil over the inside of the wok until the entire surface is lightly coated with oil. Heat the wok slowly over low heat for about 10 to 15 minutes and then wipe it thoroughly with more paper towels. The paper will become blackened. Repeat this process of coating, heating, and wiping until the paper towels come clean. With use, your wok will darken and become well seasoned, which is a good sign.

Cleaning a Wok

Once your wok has been seasoned, never scrub it with soap or water unless it has rusted. Plain, clear water is all that is needed. After each use, thoroughly dry the wok by putting it over low heat for a minute or two. If, by chance, it does rust a bit, scrub it with a cream cleanser and re-season it.

WOK ACCESSORIES

Wok Stand

This is a metal ring or frame designed to keep a conventionally shaped round-bottomed wok steady on the stove. It is essential if you want to use your wok for steaming, deep-frying, or braising.

Wok Lid

This light and inexpensive domed cover, usually made from aluminum, is used for steaming. The lid normally comes with the wok, but if not, you can purchase one separately or use any domed pot lid that fits snugly.

Spatula

A long-handled metal spatula shaped like a small shovel is ideal for scooping and tossing food in a wok. As an alternative, any good long-handled spoon can be used.

Rack

When steaming foods in your wok, you will need a wooden or metal rack or trivet to raise food above the water level. Wok sets usually include a rack, but if yours doesn't, you can buy one from an Asian grocery. Department stores and hardware shops also sell wooden and metal stands, which can serve the same purpose.

Bamboo Brush

This bundle of stiff, split bamboo is used for cleaning a wok without scrubbing off the seasoned surface. It is an attractive, inexpensive implement but it is not essential. A soft sponge will work just as well.

CLEAVERS

To Asian cooks the cleaver is an all-purpose cutting instrument that makes all other knives unnecessary. Once you gain facility with a cleaver, you will see how it can be used to slice, dice, chop, fillet, shred, or crush anything. In practice, most Asian chefs rely upon three different sizes—light, medium, and heavy—for the various cutting techniques. Of course, you may use your own familiar kitchen knives, but if you decide to invest in a cleaver, choose a good-quality stainless steel model and keep it sharpened.

STEAMERS

Steaming is an ancient cooking method used in Asia. It is a useful technique for preparing many foods of delicate taste and texture, such as fish, meats, and even soups. Bamboo steamers come in several sizes, but the 10-inch (25 cm) size is the most suitable for home use. The food is placed on a heat-proof plate that is in turn placed in the steamer. The steamer is placed in a wok or pot above boiling water; several steamers, stacked one above the other, may be utilized at once. A tight-fitting bamboo lid prevents the steam from escaping. Of course, any kind of wide, metal steamer may be used, if you prefer. Before using a bamboo steamer for the first time, wash it and then steam it empty for about 5 minutes.

SAND OR CLAY POTS

For braised dishes, soups, and cooking rice, Asians use woks and light-weight clay pots, whose design allows for the infusion of aromas and flavors into foods. Clay pots are sometimes called sand pots because of their unglazed, sandy-textured exteriors. They are available in many sizes, with matching lids, and because they are quite fragile, they are often encased in a wire frame. Use them on top of the stove (most Asian homes do not have ovens), but never put an empty sand pot on a heated element or a hot sand pot on a cold surface; the shock will crack the pot. Clay pots should always have some liquid or food in them, and when filled with food, they can take very high heat. If you use an electric stove, employ a heat-dif-fusing plate or asbestos pad to insulate the pot from direct contact with the heat. (*Note:* To avoid the release of hot steam when you lift the lid, always lift the lid away from you.)

OTHER TOOLS

Stainless steel bowls of different sizes, strainers, and colanders round out the list of basic implements. They will be very use-ful because you will often have to drain or strain oils and juices and because you will be doing much mixing of won-derful foods. It is better to have one too many tools than one too few!

Techniques

In Asian cooking, the preparation of foods and in-gredients before you begin cooking is more impor-tant and time-consuming than in any other cuisine. However, once the foundation has been prepared, the rest is comparatively quick and easy.

All ingredients must be cut into just the right shape and size. This will allow them to cook quickly and evenly while retaining their natural taste and texture. In addition, such preparation will enhance the visual appeal of whatever is being served.

CUTTING TECHNIQUES

Slicing

This is the conventional method of slicing food. Hold the food firmly on the chopping board with one hand and slice the food straight down into very thin slices. Meat is al-ways sliced across the grain to break up any fibers and to make it more tender when it is cooked. If you use a cleaver rather than a knife for this, hold the cleaver with your index finger over the far side of the top of the cleaver and keep your thumb on the side nearest you, allowing it to guide the cutting edge firmly. Hold the food with your other hand, turning your fingers under for safety. Your knuckles should act as a guide for the blade.

Horizontal or Flat Slicing

This is a technique for splitting food into two thinner pieces while retaining its overall shape, as in slicing chicken breasts or splitting shrimps. The cleaver, with its wide blade, is particularly suitable for this. Hold the blade of the cleaver or knife parallel to the chopping board. Place your free hand on top of the piece of food to keep it steady. Using a gentle cutting motion, slice sideways into the food. Depending on the recipe, you may need to repeat this process, cutting the two halves into even thinner, flat pieces.

Diagonal Slicing

This technique is used for cutting vegetables such as asparagus, carrots, or scallions (spring onions). The purpose is to expose more of the surface of the vegetable for quicker cooking. Angle the knife or cleaver at a slant and cut evenly.

Roll Cutting

This is like diagonal slicing but is used for larger vegetables such as zucchini (courgettes), large carrots, Chinese eggplant (aubergine), and Chinese white radish (daikon). As with diagonal slicing, this technique allows more of the surface of the vegetable to be exposed to the heat, thereby speeding up the cooking time. Begin by making one diagonal slice at one end of the vegetable. Then turn the vegetable 180 degrees and make the next diagonal slice. Continue in this way until you have chopped the entire vegetable into evenly sized, diamond-shaped chunks.

Shredding

This is a process like the French julienne technique by which food is cut into thin, matchstick-like shreds. First cut the food into slices. Pile several slices on top of each other and cut them *lengthwise* into fine strips. Some foods, particularly meat and chicken breasts, are easier to shred if they are first stiffened in the freezer for about 20 minutes.

Dicing

This is a simple technique of cutting food into small cubes or dice. First cut the food into slices. Stack the slices and cut them again *lengthwise* into sticks as you would for shredding. Stack the strips or sticks and cut *crosswise* into evenly sized cubes or dice.

Mincing

This is a technique to finely chop food. To mince, chefs use two cleavers, rapidly chopping with them in unison for fast results. While one cleaver or knife is easier for the novice, the process will of course take a little longer! First slice the food. Using a sharp knife or cleaver, rapidly chop the slices until the food is spread out over the chopping board. Scrape it into a pile and chop again, and continue chopping until the food reaches the desired state. You may find it easier to hold the knife or cleaver by the top of the blade (rather than by the handle) with two hands, as though you were chopping parsley. A food processor can also be used for this, but be careful not to over-mince the food or you will lose out on texture and taste.

Chopping

This is a technique used for food like whole birds or cooked food with bones, which need to be completely cut through or cut into smaller pieces. Place the food on a firm cutting surface. Use a straight, sharp, downward motion with a heavy-duty cleaver or knife. To chop through bones, hit down with the blade and then finish off the blow by pressing with the flat of your other hand on the top edge of the cleaver or knife.

Scoring

This is a technique used to pierce the surface of foods to help them cook faster and more evenly. It also gives them an attractive appearance. Use a cleaver or a sharp knife to make cuts into the food at a slight angle and to a depth of about ⅛ inch (.5 cm). (Take care not to cut all the way through.) Make cuts all over the surface of the food, cutting crisscross to give a wide, diamond-shaped pattern.

OTHER PREPARATION TECHNIQUES

Marinating

Soaking meat, fish, seafood, or poultry in a liquid such as soy sauce, rice wine, and cornstarch (cornflour) enhances the food's natural flavors and tenderizes it. You can add spices or seasonings such as sugar, chiles, five-spice powder, or Sichuan peppercorns. Marinate at least 20 minutes in order to infuse the foods properly.

Thickening

Cornstarch (cornflour) blended with cold water is frequently used to thicken sauces and glaze dishes. To prevent a lumpy glaze or sauce, always make sure the mixture is smooth and well blended before adding it.

Velveting

Velveting is used to prevent delicate foods like chicken breasts or shrimps (prawns) from overcooking. The food is coated with a mixture of egg white (unbeaten), cornstarch (cornflour), and sometimes salt. It is then refrigerated for 20 to 30 minutes to allow the coating to adhere to the food. The velvet cloak protects the flavor and texture of the food when it is put into hot oil or water.

COOKING TECHNIQUES

Blanching

Putting food into hot water or into moderately hot oil for a few minutes will cook it briefly but not entirely. It is a sort of softening-up process to prepare the food for final cooking. Chicken is often blanched in oil or water after being velveted. Meat is sometimes blanched to rid it of unwanted gristle and fat and to ensure a clean taste and appearance. It is common to blanch Asian vegetables like Chinese broccoli, Chinese white cabbage, or Napa cabbage. Plunge the vegetable into a pot of boiling water for several minutes and either serve it immediately, dressed with a sauce or plain, or drain it and plunge it into cold water to arrest the cooking process. Then stir-fry it to finish the cooking. You must always avoid overcooking your foods at the blanching stage.

Poaching

This is a method of simmering food gently until it is only partially cooked before putting it into soup or combining it with a sauce and continuing the cooking process. Delicately flavored and textured foods such as eggs and chicken are often poached.

Stir-Frying

This is the most famous of all Asian cooking techniques and possibly the trickiest. Once you have mastered it, it will become your favorite technique. Success with it depends upon having all the required ingredients prepared, measured out, and at hand, and upon having a good source of fierce heat. The advantage of stir-frying, if properly executed, is that foods can be cooked in minutes and in very little oil so that they retain their natural flavors and textures. It is very important not to overcook stir-fried foods so that they become greasy. A wok is the best pan for stir-frying because not only does its shape conduct the heat well but its high sides enable you to toss the ingredients rapidly, keeping them constantly moving while they are cooking. After preparing all the ingredients for stir-frying, the next steps are:

- Heat a wok or frying pan until it is very hot *before* adding any oil. This prevents food from sticking and ensures an even heat. Peanut oil is my favorite oil precisely because it can take this high heat without burning. When you add the oil, use a metal spatula or long-handled spoon to distribute it evenly over the surface of the pan. The oil should be very hot—almost smoking—before you add the next ingredient, unless you are going to flavor the oil with spices or ingredients like garlic, ginger, and so on (see next below).

- If you are flavoring the oil with garlic, ginger, dried red chile, or salt, add them to the oil before the oil gets so hot that it begins to smoke. (If the oil is too hot, these ingredients will burn and become bitter.) Toss them quickly in the oil for a few seconds. In some recipes these flavorings will be removed and discarded before the cooking proceeds.

- Add the ingredients as described in the recipe and proceed to stir-fry by tossing them over the surface of the wok or pan with a metal spatula or long-handled spoon. If you are stir-frying meat, let each side rest for just a few seconds before continuing to stir. Keep moving the food from the center of the wok to the sides.

- Some stir-fried dishes are thickened with a mixture of cornstarch and cold water. To avoid getting a lumpy sauce be sure to remove the wok or pan from the heat for a minute before you add the cornstarch mixture and make sure the mixture is thoroughly blended before it is added. Sauces can then be returned to the heat and thickened.

Deep-Frying

This is an important technique in Asian cookery. The trick is to regulate the heat so that the surface of the food is sealed but the food does not brown so fast that it is uncooked inside. As with any technique, mastery comes with practice. Although deep-fried food must not be greasy, the process does require a lot of oil. For deep-frying, Asians use a wok, which requires less oil.

SOME POINTS TO BEAR IN MIND
WHEN DEEP-FRYING ARE:

- Wait for the oil to get hot before adding food. The oil should give off a haze and produce little wisps of smoke when it is the right temperature. You can test it by dropping in a small piece of food. If the oil bubbles all over, it is sufficiently hot. Adjust the heat as necessary to prevent the oil from actually smoking or overheating.

- To prevent splattering, thoroughly dry the food to be deep-fried. If the food is in a marinade, remove it with a slotted spoon and let it drain before putting it into the oil. If you are using batter, make sure all the excess batter drips off before adding the food to the hot oil.

Shallow-Frying

This technique is similar to sautéing. You use more oil than you use for stir-frying but less than for deep-frying. The food is fried first on one side and then on the other. Sometimes the excess oil is drained off and a sauce added to complete the dish.

Slow-Simmering and Steeping

These processes are similar. In slow-simmering, food is immersed in a liquid that is brought almost to the boil and then the temperature is reduced so that the liquid simmers, cooking the food to the desired degree. This is the technique used for making a stock. In steeping, food is similarly immersed in liquid (usually stock) and simmered for a time. The heat is then turned off and the heat of the liquid finishes off the cooking process.

Braising and Red-Braising

This technique is most often applied to tougher cuts of meat and certain vegetables. The food is usually browned and then put into a stock that has been flavored with seasonings and spices. After the stock is brought to the boil, the heat is reduced and the food is simmered gently until it is cooked. Red-braising is simply the technique by which food is braised in a dark liquid, such as soy sauce. This gives food a reddish brown color. This type of braising sauce can be frozen for reuse. It can be reused many times and becomes richer in flavor every time.

Steaming

Along with stir-frying and deep-frying, steaming is the most widely used technique. Steamed foods are cooked by a gentle, moist heat that circulates freely in order to cook the food. It is an excellent method for bringing out subtle flavors and therefore is particularly appropriate for fish or poultry.

SOME DIFFERENT METHODS
OF STEAMING ARE:

- *Using a bamboo steamer in a wok.* For this you need a large bamboo steamer about 10 inches (25 cm) wide. Pour about

2 inches (5 cm) of water into a wok and bring it to a simmer. Put the bamboo steamer containing the food into the wok, where it should rest safely perched on the sloping sides. Cover the steamer with its lid, and steam the food until it is cooked. Replenish the water as required.

- *Using a wok as a steamer.* Pour about 2 inches (5 cm) of water into a wok. Put a metal or wooden rack into the wok. Bring the water to a simmer and put the food to be steamed onto a plate. Lower the plate onto the rack and cover the wok tightly with a wok lid. Check the water level from time to time and replenish it with hot water when necessary. The water should never make direct contact with the food.

- *Using a large roasting pan or pot as a steamer.* Put a metal or wooden rack into the pan or pot and pour in about 2 inches (5 cm) of water. Bring it to a simmer and put the food to be steamed onto a plate. Lower the plate onto the rack and cover the pan or pot with a lid or with aluminum foil. Replenish the water as necessary.

Roasting

In Asia, because most homes do not have ovens, roasting is done only in commercial establishments. These commercial places usually roast food in large, metal, drum-shaped ovens that stand about 5 feet (1.5 m) high and are fueled by charcoal. The food is hung on hooks inside the oven over intense heat. The idea is to expose all of the surface of the food to the heat to give it a crisp outer surface with a moist interior.

Barbecuing

This variation on roasting is not very common. Marinated meat is placed over a charcoal fire, and the meat is constantly basted to keep it moist. Modern grills and outdoor barbecues produce much the same result.

Twice-Cooking

As the name implies, this is a two-step process involving two quite different techniques, such as simmering and stir-frying. It is used to change the texture of food, to infuse it with flavor, and to render foods manageable that are difficult to cook. The process is especially useful for removing fat from meat before final cooking.

VEGETABLES

AMARANTH

(Amaranthus gangeticus; also A. tricolor and A. oleraceus)

This leafy vegetable is also known as **Chinese spinach** or **red-in-the-snow cabbage**. It is an ancient food mentioned in early Chinese records and is eaten throughout Asia. In Greek mythology, the plant was held to be immortal and thus Helen of Troy was described as being of "amaranthine" beauty. There are two varieties: one with very green leaves, the other with leaves tinged with purple and red. Amaranth is hardy, arriving in early spring, when it peeks through the snow that is still on the ground. Hence, its name is most apt, for its red crimson leaves contrast with the snowy field.

Amaranth is salt-pickled as well as eaten fresh. The pickled variety adds a pungent, slightly sour but not unpleasant taste to dishes when used as a flavoring. It can also be used as an interestingly textured vegetable ingredient in stir-fried and braised dishes. The fresh variety has a wonderful green, pungent, earthy taste and flavor, rather like watercress. It is customarily stir-fried or used in soup—in fact, it is used much like spinach and can be substituted in any spinach recipe. The leaves and stems are rich in protein, iron, calcium, and vitamins A and C.

The pickled version can be purchased in cans at Chinese markets or grocers. The best brands are from China and Taiwan: all are recommended. When purchasing the fresh version, look for the variety with green leaves. Look for fresh, young leaves and stems.

Fresh amaranth should be eaten immediately, as the leaves become limp soon after they are picked. They will keep in the vegetable bin of your refrigerator for up to a day if wrapped in paper towels and placed in a plastic bag. The canned variety lasts indefinitely in the refrigerator.

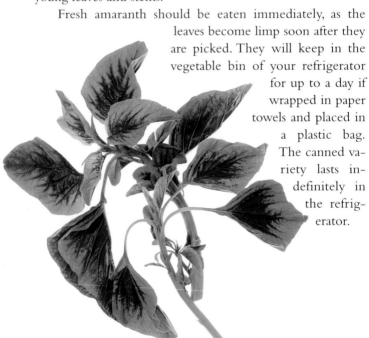

BAMBOO SHOOTS
(Dendrocalamus asper)

The bamboo plant, native to Asia, makes an invaluable contribution to life in all Asian countries except India. While its woody stems and broad leaves are used in housing construction, its softer leaves serve as protective garments and food wrappers. It is made into cooking and eating utensils as well as astrological, religious, and ceremonial paraphernalia; furniture; storage containers; and luggage. Bamboo shells were the first paper to be used to record China's history.

As if this indispensable plant were not already offering enough, its fresh young shoots were also discovered to be a food with a unique, slightly acidic flavor and a crunchy texture. Fresh bamboo shoots are easily recognizable: cylindrical spikes of overlaid greenish and yellowish papery leaves that come to a point at the top. The leaves must be removed to reveal the familiar buff-colored shoot, with its fibrous texture.

There are more than one hundred different types of bamboo, but only about ten are marketed for their edible shoots. They fall into two broad categories: spring and winter shoots. The winter shoots are smaller and more tender than the spring ones, which tend to be quite large and more fibrous. Fresh bamboo shoots are expensive and only found seasonally in markets in China, although on occasion they can also be found fresh in some Chinese grocers in the West. However, canned ones are available in the West and are more reasonably priced.

Unpeeled bamboo shoots can be stored in the refrigerator for at least a week. Peeled and parboiled, either prepared at home or purchased ready made from specialist Chinese markets, they will keep only 1 or 2 days in a plastic bag or up to 5 in a container of water. They can be frozen, but the texture will become more fibrous. Canned bamboo shoots should be transferred to a container of water once the can has been opened. These may be kept in the refrigerator for up to 6 days if the water is changed daily.

NOTES:

- Fresh bamboo shoots contain a toxin, hydrocyanic acid, which must be eliminated by blanching. Slice off the leafy husk and base of the shoot and discard. Cook the shoots whole or in chunks for at least 5 minutes, or until they no longer taste bitter. Drain, rinse, and store in cold water.

- Canned bamboo shoots tend to be pale yellow with a crunchy texture and, in some cases, a slightly sweet flavor. They come peeled and either whole or thickly sliced. Rinse them thoroughly and blanch them for 2 minutes in boiling water before use. Sliced bamboo shoots braised in soy sauce with spices is another readily available canned product that can be added to various dishes as a strong-flavored seasoning vegetable.

BITTER MELON
(MOMORDICA CHARANTIA)

This unusual vegetable requires an acquired taste. It has as many opponents as it has fans, even among the Chinese, but those who love it insist that it is worth the effort to appreciate its taste.

Bitter melon has a bumpy dark to pale green skin, and has a slightly bitter quinine flavor that has a cooling effect in one's mouth. Not surprisingly, it was originally prized for its supposed medicinal qualities: something so bitter had to be good medicine! This tropical vegetable's fibrous seed core is usually cut away, leaving a thin ring of flesh. It is used in soups, stir-fried, and steamed, as well as quick braised. A popular preparation, which reduces its bitterness, is to stuff it with seasoned pork and then steam it. It is often paired with pungent ingredients, such as black beans, garlic, or chile, which help to tone down the melon's bitterness. In some parts of China it is often dried and used as medicine. It is also thought to purify the blood and to cool one's digestive system. The greener the melon, the more bitter its taste, and most cooks wisely look for the milder, yellow-green varieties.

Store in the bottom of your refrigerator in a loose plastic or paper bag. It can keep there for about 3 to 5 days, depending on the condition in which it was bought.

NOTE:

To use, cut in half, seed, and discard interior membrane. Then, to lessen its bitter taste, either blanch or salt it, according to the instructions in the recipe.

BOK CHOY
(BRASSICA CHINENSIS)

Also called **Chinese white cabbage,** bok choy (or pak choi) is a nutritious and versatile vegetable. It has been grown in China since ancient times. Although there are many varieties (in Hong Kong alone, twenty kinds are available), the most common and most popular is the one with a long, smooth, milky white stem and large, crinkly, dark green leaves found in most supermarkets today. Other variations from the bok choy family include choy sum (Chinese flowering cabbage) (see page 22) and Shanghai bok choy (see page 40).

Bok choy has a light, fresh, slightly mustardy taste and requires little cooking. In China, it is used in soup or stir-fried with meats or simply blanched. When cooked, the leaves have a robust, almost spinach-like flavor, while the stalks are sweet and mild with a refreshing taste. Bok choy is often said to resemble Swiss chard (silverbeet) in taste; however, in fact, it is not only milder than chard but also juicier—and much more popular!

Look for firm crisp stalks and unblemished leaves. The size of the plant indicates how tender it is. The smaller the better, especially in the summer, when the hot weather toughens the stalks. Look at the bottom of the stalk; if it has a hole, it means that the bok choy is old and fibrous, and best avoided.

If you store bok choy wrapped tightly in paper towels in

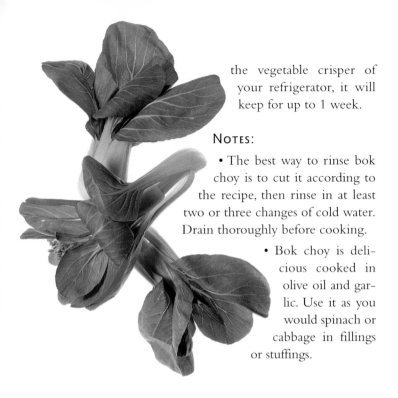

the vegetable crisper of your refrigerator, it will keep for up to 1 week.

NOTES:

• The best way to rinse bok choy is to cut it according to the recipe, then rinse in at least two or three changes of cold water. Drain thoroughly before cooking.

• Bok choy is delicious cooked in olive oil and garlic. Use it as you would spinach or cabbage in fillings or stuffings.

CHILES
(CAPSICUM FRUTESCENS)

Archaeological records suggest that chiles were eaten in Mexico nine thousand years ago and were cultivated two thousand years later. They were introduced to Asia around 100 to 150 years ago from the Americas. There are two varieties: the bell peppers (capsicums), which are very mild and sweet, and the hot peppers, known as chiles. There are many different types of hot chiles, varying in size, shape, color, and intensity or "hotness." In Chinese cuisine, fresh chiles are stuffed or eaten whole. They are used to make sauce or paste and are pickled and preserved for use in stir-fried and braised dishes. Chiles are also dry-roasted to add a special pungent smoky flavor. Dried chiles are used in countless forms, ground, whole, or as a powder. In China, fresh chiles are small and generally red, but there are also green varieties. Their taste is mildly spicy and pungent. Smaller varieties can be found, but the larger, longer ones are the ones most available. They are popular not only for color and presentation as garnishes but also for the zest they add to many dishes and sauces.

Try the varieties available in your local markets. People's tastes vary and some chiles are very hot, so it is important that you find the chiles that best suit your palate. Look for firm, fresh chiles that are bright, with no brown patches or black spots. Use red chiles wherever possible, as they are generally milder than green ones because they sweeten as they ripen.

Store in the vegetable crisper of your refrigerator. Chiles should keep for at least 1 week.

NOTE:

To prepare fresh chiles, first rinse them in cold water. Using a small, sharp knife, slit them lengthwise. Remove and discard the seeds. Rinse the chiles well under cold, running water, and then prepare them according to the instructions in the recipe. Wash your hands, the knife, and the chopping board before preparing other foods, and be careful not to touch your eyes until you have washed your hands thoroughly with soap and water.

CHINESE BROCCOLI
(BRASSICA ALBOGLABRA)

This highly nutritious green leafy plant with smooth, round stems and small, white flowers is sometimes called **Chinese kale**. That name should tell you that it is not quite the same thing as Chinese broccoli but resembles Swiss chard (silverbeet). It is a delicious vegetable that is earthy in taste and slightly bitter, perhaps the price to pay for its being so rich in calcium, iron, and vitamins A and C.

Chinese broccoli is usually prepared by blanching in salted water and serving with oyster sauce—it has character enough to go well with that distinctively flavored condiment. It also works well in stir-fries with meats, to be served with noodles and soups. Use Chinese broccoli the way you would use regular broccoli, kale, Swiss chard, and grape seed greens.

Buy stems which are firm and leaves that look fresh and deep olive green. It should be stored in a plastic bag in the vegetable crisper of the refrigerator where it will keep for several days.

CHINESE CELERY
(Apium graveolens)

Chinese celery probably evolved from a wild form of Asian celery. It is heartier than the one familiar to Western kitchens. In China, celery has a long history of use as a flavoring herb and vegetable, and is one of the most widely grown vegetables there. Indeed, even outside of China, celery is one of the staples of the world's cuisine because of the way it very effectively (and cheaply) extends the vegetable content of any recipe. I won't even mention the usefulness of the celery stalk or rib as a swizzle stick in a Bloody Mary!

Unlike the Western variety, Chinese celery stalks are thin, hollow, and very crisp, with colors varying from white to dark green. (Technically, the entire celery bunch is the stalk and the individual branches are ribs.) The meager crown of head leaves of Chinese celery is similar to that of the European variety. Both the stems and stalks of Chinese celery have a strong flavor. Whereas it is most commonly stir-fried, it is also used in soups and braised dishes. Store as you would any celery in the lower part of your refrigerator. It should keep for several days.

CHINESE CHIVES
(Allium tuberosum)

Chives, garlic, and shallots are closely allied to onions. Each has its own distinctive flavor that makes it a valued addition to many recipes, especially to stir-fried dishes. Chives are mild, small versions of the onion. Having no bulb, only the green shoots are eaten. In China, which has relatively few food herbs (medicinal herbs are abundant), garlic chives are very popular as a flavoring herb. With their stronger flavor they are preferred in stuffings as well as in stir-fried dishes and soups.

There are several variations of this chive: Yellow chives are distinctly, if mildly, onion flavored. Their yellow color and mild taste come from their being grown out of direct sunlight. Flowering chives have hollow stems topped by a flower bud. The tough ends are chopped off and the remainder is consumed as a vegetable.

Green chives have a distinctive pungency that adds richness to stir-fried dishes. Buy them fresh at Chinese markets or grocers. They should be fresh-looking, not wilted and tired. Flowering chives will be stiff and aromatic. Yellow chives are limp and should not have brown edges. Garlic and green chives should be deep green and fresh-looking.

Wash and dry thoroughly and store between paper towels in a plastic bag in the lower part of your refrigerator for only 2 days, as they are highly perishable. Most will remain fresh for at least 2 days; however, yellow chives are extremely fragile and will keep for only 1 day.

NOTE:
To prepare, select the freshest leaves possible, trim away any decaying parts, and proceed with your recipe.

CHINESE FLOWERING CABBAGE

(BRASSICA CHINENSIS VAR. PARACHINENSIS)

In their marvelously successful effort to provide themselves with nutritious sustenance, the Chinese people have gladly and imaginatively exploited every food resource available to them. Among the most beneficial means to that end is their reliance on a vast number of different vegetable greens, the unique source of so many essential vitamins, minerals, and trace elements. Chinese flowering cabbage is but one, albeit very important, example of this dietary proclivity.

The cabbage family of vegetables used in China is actually almost unknown in the rest of the world, except as it has spread from China with emigrating populations. It would be tedious to list all of the types that are cultivated and consumed in enormous quantities every day in China; it is safe to say, however, that Chinese flowering cabbage is among the most popular. A relative of another favorite green, bok choy, this cabbage is slimmer with yellow flowers to complement its green leaves.

This vegetable is delicious stir-fried with olive oil and garlic and used in fillings and with pasta. The cabbage leaves require little cooking to bring out their delicate, sweet, mustard flavor. The leaves also make a mustardy salad green; however, they need to be washed well. The best way to prepare the leaves is to trim and cut them and then rinse them several times in cold water.

Look for firm stalks and check the stems to make sure they are not old and fibrous. They should look fresh and be without brown spots.

Store in the vegetable crisper of the refrigerator. Like bok choy, it should keep for about 1 week.

CHINESE LEEK
(ALLIUM RAMOSUM)

This vegetable is grown and used primarily in northern China, where it is treated as an onion and stir-fried with meats. In the West, except among the Welsh, the leek is often regarded as the poor relative of its cousins, the asparagus and the onion. This is unfair because the leek possesses notable dietary riches.

The European leek, of Mediterranean origin and already a standard by the time of King Richard II in the late fourteenth century, is larger with a more fibrous texture than the Chinese leek. The Chinese leek's pungent and slightly acidic flavor sweetens with cooking. To quote one authority: "It has a warm character," and its nutritional virtues are matched by its medicinal potency. One Ming Dynasty herbalist listed it first among important vegetable medicines, noting that "it restores the spirit and calms the five viscera." No one has ever claimed as much for asparagus or onions!

The young leeks available in season at organic food stores and in some Chinese markets are a good substitute for Chinese leeks, which are currently not available outside of China. Look for firm stalks without brown or yellow spots.

To use, cut off and discard the green tops and roots and slice the leek in half lengthwise. Wash them well. Put them in a plastic bag wrapped with paper towels and store them in the vegetable crisper of your refrigerator, where they should keep for at least 5 days.

CHINESE LONGBEANS
(VIGNA SESQUIPEDALIS)

Also known as **Chinese pea, snake bean,** and **asparagus pea** (or **asparagus bean**), these beans either originated in China or were introduced there in prehistoric times. Sometimes they are called yard-long beans, as they grow as long as 3 feet (1 m). They are very popular and, in season, may be found in great abundance in every Chinese market. They add significant calories and vegetable protein to the Chinese diet.

Quite unrelated to our familiar green beans, they are neither crisp nor sweet, although they do have a crunchy texture. Because they have a mild, subtle taste, they are best when combined with more assertively flavored foods. There are two varieties: the pale green type and the dark green, thinner type. In China, the beans are chopped and then stir-fried with meats or fermented bean curd. Because they cook rapidly, they're very suitable for stir-fry recipes. The Cantonese often cook them with black beans or fermented bean curd. In Sichuan, they are deep-fried, drained, and then paired with chiles and garlic.

Buy beans that are firm and fresh, with no dark marks. You will usually find beans sold in looped bunches, so there is no need to string them before cooking.

Store the fresh beans in a plastic bag in the refrigerator and use within 4 days.

CHINESE MUSTARD CABBAGE
(BRASSICA JUNCEA)

Also known as **gaai choy,** these mustard plants are not the same thing as cabbages, but they are very similar in appearance, nutritional value, and popularity. With rice and soybeans, mustard plants and cabbages have been the poor people's basic diet for many centuries. Preserved with chiles or pickled in brine or sugar, mustard cabbages are eaten throughout the year. When in season and fresh, they can be simply stir-fried with ginger and salt. They are also used in soups, to which they impart flavor and astringency. Young, fresh mustard cabbages are tender throughout and are consumed in their entirety. They are a good source of vitamins and of minerals such as calcium.

Pick mustard cabbage that has firm broad leaves without discoloration. Avoid limp and tired-looking cabbage. Stems should be firm and without holes, which indicate age and a fibrous texture.

Stored in the vegetable crisper of your refrigerator, Chinese mustard cabbage should last for at least 5 days.

NOTE:
Cut the mustard greens into pieces before washing in several changes of cold water.

CHINESE WHITE RADISH
(RAPHANUS SATIVUS)

Chinese white radish is also known as **Chinese icicle radish** or as **mooli,** or by its Japanese name, **daikon.** It is long, white, and rather like a carrot in shape but usually much larger. It is a winter radish or root that can withstand long cooking without disintegrating or losing its distinctive radish taste and texture. In ancient times, it was valued as a food and as a medicine—although some avoided it because it allegedly induced hiccups.

In China, these radishes are usually found in homemade dishes, treated the way Western cooks use potatoes or carrots. They are never used without being peeled because most of the hot flavor is in the skin, and when peeled the radish becomes mild tasting. They are not only cooked but are also pickled or salted and dried to preserve them. They are crisp-textured and tender when cooked and vary in flavor from sweet and mild to fairly hot and pungent. The stronger flavored variety is used for pickles, the milder for cooking. Like turnips, these radishes are most often stir-fried, braised, boiled, or steamed and then combined with pork or beef. The milder radish can even be made into a savory pudding for dim sum. Unlike most root vegetables, these radishes are light and refreshing, not heavy and starchy.

Look for the firm, heavy, solid, and unblemished ones. They should be slightly translucent inside, with solid, smooth skin outside. Avoid the very large ones, which tend to be fibrous. You can find them in some supermarkets and almost always at Chinese or Asian markets.

Store in a plastic bag in the vegetable crisper of your refrigerator, where they will keep for over a week.

NOTE:

Use the radish as you would turnips, carrots, or potatoes. It absorbs the sauces in which it is cooked as it becomes tender.

CORIANDER
(CORIANDRUM SATIVUM)

Fresh coriander (also known as **Chinese parsley** or **cilantro**) is one of the relatively few food herbs in the Chinese lexicon. It is a standard in southern China and has been used there since 200 BC. It looks like flat parsley, but its pungent, musky, citrus-like character gives it an unmistakable flavor. Believed to have calming properties, it was also valued as a medicinal agent. Its feathery leaves are often used as a garnish, or the herb is chopped and mixed into sauces and stuffings. It helps moderate rich flavors, its own flavors being strong, earthy, and fresh.

When buying fresh coriander, look for deep green, fresh-looking leaves. Yellow and limp leaves indicate age and should be avoided.

If you buy fresh coriander with roots, stand the coriander in water. Otherwise, to store fresh coriander, wash it in cold water, drain it thoroughly or spin dry in a salad spinner, and put it in a clean plastic bag with a couple of sheets of moist paper towel. Stored in the vegetable crisper of your refrigerator, it will keep for several days.

NOTE:

You may mix coriander with basil for an Asian pesto-style flavoring for noodles.

EGGPLANT
(Solanum melongena)

Named after the white-skinned variety, which was the first that English-speaking people encountered, the eggplant is a popular and inexpensive food found throughout China. This versatile vegetable (also known as **aubergine**) may be found in ivory, purple, or even light green. It is native to India and Southeast Asia and has been cultivated in China since 600 BC. The original Chinese name translates as "Malayan purple melon," indicating that Chinese traders brought it from the Malay peninsula. Although it is botanically a fruit, it is consumed as a vegetable. The size and shape varies from large and plump to small and thin. The most common type, the large purple variety, is available in most supermarkets; the Chinese prefer the more delicate flavor of the small, thin eggplant, and these are becoming more available in the West.

Try to find the long, thin, light purple variety known as Chinese or Japanese eggplant. They look like young zucchini (courgettes) and tend to be sweet and tender with very little seeds.

Look for eggplants with unwrinkled, firm, and unblemished skin. They should have a hollow sound when tapped. The large variety found in supermarkets can be kept unwrapped in the bottom part of your refrigerator for at least 2 weeks. However, the thinner, Chinese variety should be eaten within a few days of purchase.

Notes:

The Chinese normally don't peel their eggplants because the skin preserves texture, taste, and shape. Large eggplants should be cut according to the recipe, sprinkled with a little salt, and left to sit for 20 minutes. They should then

be rinsed and any liquid blotted dry with paper towels. This process extracts bitter juices and excess moisture from the vegetable before it is cooked, giving a truer taste to a dish. The eggplant also absorbs less moisture after this process. This procedure is unnecessary if you are using Chinese eggplants.

GARLIC
(ALLIUM SATIVUM)

The English word garlic comes from the Anglo-Saxon word meaning "spear plant." This is an apt description for the straight, branchless stems characteristic of the subfamily of the lily to which garlic belongs, along with leeks, scallions or spring onions, shallots, and onions.

True garlic is not found in the wild, the plant having been domesticated thousands of years ago in central Asia. The Chinese have been cultivating garlic since at least 3000 BC, and Chinese cuisine is inconceivable without its distinct, sweet, pungent, aromatic contribution. Cooks often smash a clove of garlic into hot cooking oil; this "sweetens" the oil and gives it a bracing aroma. Once its essence is captured by the oil, the garlic husk is removed and discarded. Whether whole, chopped, minced, crushed, pickled, boiled, smoked, in flavored oils and spicy sauces, by itself, or with other robust ingredients such as black beans, curry, shrimp paste, scallions, or ginger, garlic is an essential and revered element in the Chinese culinary diet.

Scientists have recently begun to take seriously the alleged magical and medicinal qualities of garlic. Herbalists and traditional folk healers have always maintained that garlic is both a preventer and a healer of disease. Recent scientific studies now indicate that there may be a factual basis to their beliefs. Controlled experiments have led many researchers to conclude that the consumption of garlic lowers the risk of stomach cancer, fights off harmful cholesterol, lowers blood pressure, and reduces the incidence of unhealthy blood clotting. Garlic consists of over two hundred chemical compounds in unstable balance and such chemicals may readily perform therapeutic functions. We now know, for example, that the compound diallyl disulfide, which is the major source of garlic's odor, is also one of the most active chemopreventive agents known to science. All of these claims need further scientific analysis; in the meantime, we should simply enjoy the culinary virtues of one of nature's greatest gifts to our palates.

The true garlic flavor is released by chemical reactions that occur when the garlic cells are broken. Garlic flavor is

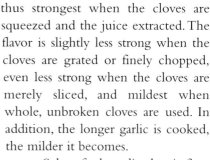

thus strongest when the cloves are squeezed and the juice extracted. The flavor is slightly less strong when the cloves are grated or finely chopped, even less strong when the cloves are merely sliced, and mildest when whole, unbroken cloves are used. In addition, the longer garlic is cooked, the milder it becomes.

Select fresh garlic that is firm and heavy. Cloves that are pinkish in color seem to have better flavor.

Garlic should be stored in a cool, dry place but not in the refrigerator, where it can easily become mildewed or begin sprouting.

NOTES:

• Peeling garlic cloves is laborious. Try this Chinese technique: Boil the garlic cloves with the skins on for 2 minutes and then leave them in the hot water for 5 minutes. The skins will come off quite easily. (The cooking does mute the intensity of the garlic.) The other trick is to bruise the cloves with the side of a Chinese cleaver or heavy kitchen knife. The skins will break away.

• If the garlic begins to sprout, cut the cloves in half and remove the central greenish core before preceding with the preparation of the garlic.

• Keep chopped garlic in oil to prevent it from oxidizing and growing bitter.

Garlic Shoots

As the name indicates, these are young shoots of garlic that precede the formation of the garlic bulb. And, as might be expected, garlic shoots have a mild and refreshing flavor with a delicate aroma, a combination that is highly prized among discerning gourmets. The shoots look like and are used in the manner of scallions, with their green tops serving either as a garnish or flavoring.

Like scallions, they should be firm and green looking without any brown spots. Their fragrance indicates their freshness. They are usually available during a brief time each year, in the spring or before each garlic harvest.

Keep in the bottom part of your refrigerator. They should be used within 2 days.

GINGER
(ZINGIBER OFFICINALE)

Ginger belongs to the small subfamily of spices that also includes cardamom (seeds) and turmeric, and that is native to southern Asia. The name ginger derives from a Sanskrit term that means "horn-shaped," a reference to one of the common natural shapes of this "rhizome" or underground stem. Ginger is one of the five "ancient" spices of Chinese cookery, along with red pepper, scallions (spring onions), garlic, and cinnamon. The Chinese have been exploiting its virtues since 600 BC, both as a spice and as a medicinal food. In its latter role ginger is believed to soothe one's intestines, ward off the common cold, and do wonders for one's sexual and gustatorial appetites. It appears that ginger was introduced to Western Europe early in the Middle Ages and it soon became one of the most popular or, at least, abundant spices in use.

Ginger is golden beige in color, with a thin, dry skin. Whether whole, sliced, ground into a powder, pickled, or candied, ginger preserves its peculiar fragrance and taste, giving a rich dimension to any recipe of which it is a part. It has a "clean" taste that adds subtlety to delicate dishes like fried seafood and counterbalances more robust dishes like beef and pork. Local boosters claim that the most aromatic and most potent ginger is to be found in Guangzhou (Canton), but throughout China ginger is used in all sorts of recipes including soups, sauces, and flavored beverages. In China, fresh ginger is often shredded into light soups and added to marinades. Small wonder it is as ubiquitous as garlic in Chinese cuisine.

In India and Pakistan, and throughout southern Asia, ginger is an essential element in almost every traditional dish, whether a soup, vegetable, fish and seafood, meat, curry, sauce, or rice dish. In Europe, ginger has most often been used in pastries, cookies, and other sweet treats. In recent years, however, European chefs, influenced by their Asian colleagues, have been utilizing this versatile spice in main course recipes with great effectiveness.

Fortunately, fresh ginger is now widely available. Older, more shriveled ginger is used for medicinal broths. However, for most culinary purposes, you want to look for ginger that is firm, smooth, and clear-skinned. Avoid fibrous, large ginger.

Young-stem ginger often makes a seasonal appearance in the markets of China, but is hard to find in the West. These are knobby-looking and a kind of moist pink, looking rather naked. This is the newest spring growth of ginger and is usually stir-fried and eaten in various dishes; it is also commonly pickled in China. Because it is so tender, it does not need peeling and can be eaten as a vegetable. A popular way to eat pickled young ginger is with preserved "thousand-year-old" duck eggs as a snack. It is often served in restaurants or private homes as an hors d'oeuvre.

Very young, pale yellow ginger should be used within 2 days of purchase, while the older ginger, if wrapped with a paper towel and then in plastic wrap, will keep in the refrigerator for up to 2 weeks. Peeled ginger covered in rice wine or dry sherry refrigerated in a glass jar will last for several months.

This has the added benefit of producing a flavored wine that can be substituted in recipes. Ginger should *never* be frozen.

Notes:

- To extract ginger juice, which can be used in marinades to give a subtle ginger taste without the bite of the fresh, chopped pieces, cut unpeeled ginger into 1-inch (2.5 cm-) chunks and drop them into a food processor that's running. When the ginger is finely chopped, squeeze out the juice by hand through a cotton or linen towel. Another method is to mash the ginger with a kitchen mallet or the side of a cleaver or knife until most of the fibers are exposed. Then simply squeeze out the juice by hand through a cotton or linen towel. Alternatively, you could place a piece of fresh ginger and 2 tablespoons (30 ml) of water in a blender, liquefy, and then strain the juice.

- Use ginger peel to flavor oil before stir-frying.

- Ginger usually should be peeled before using.

JICAMA
(Pachyrhizus erosus)

Also known as **yam bean,** jicama resembles the type of sweet potato found in the American south. It is a New World plant that originally came from a Mexican variety of the morning-glory vine. Carried to Asia about three hundred years ago, it is very popular in southern China, where it is mainly grown for its large, fleshy, four-lobed tuber.

It is a slightly sweet and crunchy vegetable that adds a refreshing quality to many recipes. It is similar in taste and usages to another tuber—the water chestnut. In fact, it is often recommended as a substitute for fresh water chestnuts. It can be blanched, stir-fried, boiled, and even deep-fried. It is also popular in parts of Southeast Asia.

Jicama will keep for at least a week in the lower part of your refrigerator. It should be peeled just before use.

LEMONGRASS
(Cymbopogon citratus)

This Southeast Asian original is not often used in China, and usually only in dried form for making tea. Its subtle lemony fragrance and flavor impart a very special aroma to delicate foods, and it is a standard ingredient in Thai and Vietnamese dishes. As is typical in Asian cuisine, the herb is considered a medicinal agent as well as a spice and is often prescribed for digestive disorders.

Lemongrass is closely related to citronella grass. The latter plant has a stronger oil content and is more likely to be used commercially in perfumes and as a mosquito repellant. The two relatives should not be confused.

Fresh lemongrass is sold in stalks that can be 2 feet (.6 m) long and look like very long scallions. It is a fibrous plant, but this is no problem because what it is used for is its fragrance and taste. The lemongrass pieces are always removed after the dish is cooked. Some recipes may call for the lemongrass to be finely chopped or pounded into a paste, in which case it becomes an integral part of the dish.

Lemongrass is usually found in Chinese or other Asian markets. Get it as fresh as possible. Avoid using dried lemongrass for cooking: it is mostly used in herbal tea.

It can be kept wrapped loosely in a plastic bag in the bottom part of your refrigerator for up to 1 week.

NOTES:

• To use, pound the bulb end of the stalk and trim the tough outer leaves. Use only the tender inner core.

• Lemon is not a substitute for the flavor of lemongrass.

LOTUS ROOT
(Nelumbo nucifera)

This well-known, perennial aquatic plant with its beautiful white and pink water-lily flowers is a native of Asia. Although the whole lotus plant is edible, the root or stems are the parts most commonly available. They are buff-colored, wooden-looking long roots that are divided into sausage-like segments of up to 5 inches (22 cm) each. The roots have a crispy fibrous texture with a mild, distinctive flavor. (Some say they resemble artichokes.) They may be cooked in many ways: stir-fried, mixed with other vegetables, used in vegetarian dishes, dried, steamed in soup, fried, or candied. Sliced and deep-fried they make a wonderful-looking garnish. They are also used raw in salads and cut into slices to make a most attractive display. They also provide a specialty starch.

Look for lotus roots that are firm and free of bruises.

Uncut, they can be kept in the bottom part of your refrigerator for up to 3 weeks.

PEA SHOOTS
(Pisum sativum)

The delicate, tender leaves from snow pea (mange tout) or garden pea plants. They have a subtle, delectable flavor, like young spinach, and are commonly stir-fried or used in soup.

Look for fresh shoots that are not wilted at all, and use them the day you buy them.

PEKING CABBAGE
(Brassica pekinensis)

The Chinese have no word that corresponds to our word vegetable. The word *cai,* however, which means "greens" (or leaves and stems of vegetables), is generalized to cover many food plants. There are four other words for root and tuber plants and for fruits and nuts. But *cai* is the most important category because it includes the vegetables that, with grains and soybeans, are the most characteristic and abundant foods in the Chinese diet. Preeminent among the *cai* foods are cabbages.

All types of cabbages cultivated in China are more nutritious than the common European varieties. All of them have a mild taste, but Peking cabbages, also known as **Napa cabbages**, are the mildest: they are sweet, not bitter or mustardy. They have been cultivated for over fifteen hundred years because they are very rich in vitamins, minerals, and fiber. In this regard, they are more like broccoli than our cabbages. Peking cabbages have delightfully crisp, fibrous leaves, which is why they are often called "celery cabbages."

Because of the regional and climatic differences, Peking cabbages come in various shapes and sizes, from long, barrel shaped specimens to fat, squat types. Their leaves are firm and tightly packed and pale green (sometimes slightly yellow) in color. They look most like our romaine (cos) lettuce.

This versatile *cai* is used in soups and in stir-fried meat dishes. Its leaves, which readily absorb flavors, and its sweet, pleasant taste make it a favorite match for foods with a rich flavor. It is used as a salad green, and it is also enjoyed pickled with salt and chiles.

Look for fresh cabbage that is not wilted. It should have a crisp look with no yellow or brown spots.

Wrapped loosely in paper towels in the lower part of your refrigerator, it should last up to 1 week.

NOTE:

• Do not boil this cabbage. It is rather delicate and fragile. Slow, gentle cooking brings out its sweet flavor. Every part of the cabbage can be used.

SCALLIONS
(ALLIUM FISTULOSUM)

Also known as **spring onions** or **green onions** and extensively grown and used throughout Asia, the scallion is probably Asia's most universally used vegetable and seasoning ingredient. The flavor is milder and more subtle than the onion and it cooks quickly, making it suitable for stir-fried dishes. Except for the short, stringy roots, all parts of the scallion, from the green top to the white bulb, are used. In ancient China, young scallions were pickled and preserved for consumption during the winter months. Scallions are used often in combination with garlic and ginger and are sometimes added at the very end of the cooking process to preserve the color and flavor of the scallion. Because they are crunchy and mild flavored, they don't need much cooking.

Look for firm, clean-looking scallions. Avoid any yellowish ones. If kept wrapped in paper towels in the lower part of your refrigerator, they should keep for several days.

NOTE:

- Scallions are known as shallots in Louisiana, which can confuse a recipe.

SHALLOTS
(Allium cepa)

Shallots are mild-flavored members of the onion family that are used extensively in Southeast Asian cooking and to a lesser extent in Chinese cooking. They grow in clusters of small bulbs, each no larger than a golf ball, and often much smaller, with thin, copper-red skins and white flesh with hints of violet and red. They have a distinct onion taste without being as strong or as tear-inducing as ordinary onions. Shallots are similar to another small onion that is also used in China. These onions grow wild in the mountains of Kiangsi and are widely cultivated as well. As shallots are so readily available in the West, they make an excellent substitute for the Chinese wild onion. In China, you will find fresh or pickled shallots served with preserved eggs as a snack. They are also excellent in sauces, soups, stir-fries, and braised dishes—anywhere a gentler onion flavor is desired.

Shallots are available fresh or freeze-dried in most supermarkets. Peel, slice, or chop fresh shallots as you would onions. Freeze-dried onions should be reconstituted according to the package directions before use. Look for firm shallots with no soft or brown spots. They should not be sprouting.

Keep them in a cool, dry place (do not refrigerate). Fresh shallots should keep for up to a month; freeze-dried shallots should keep for as long as six months.

SHANGHAI BOK CHOY
(Brassica chinensis)

Also known as **baby bok choy**, this is a miniature version of bok choy (see page 17). It is delicious in soups or stir-fries, braised whole, or simply blanched.

Shanghai bok choy is available in Asian markets and in some supermarkets. Look for firm, unblemished leaves.

Wrap it tightly in paper towels and store in your refrigerator, and Shanghai bok choy will keep for up to a week.

SILK SQUASH
(Luffa acutangula)

Also called **angles luffa** or **Chinese okra**, this is a popular vegetable found in markets throughout China. It is a long, thin squash that tapers at one end with deep, narrow ridges. Because it grows bitter with age, it is eaten when young. It is very similar to the zucchini (courgette) in texture, with a wonderful earthy flavor. Some people find a similarity in taste and texture to okra, hence it has been called Chinese okra.

To use, peel away the tough ridges. You may leave on some of the green. The inside flesh turns soft and tender as it cooks, tasting finally like a cross between a cucumber and zucchini. Being absorbent, it readily picks up the flavors of the sauce or food it is cooked with. It is usually stir-fried or deep-fried.

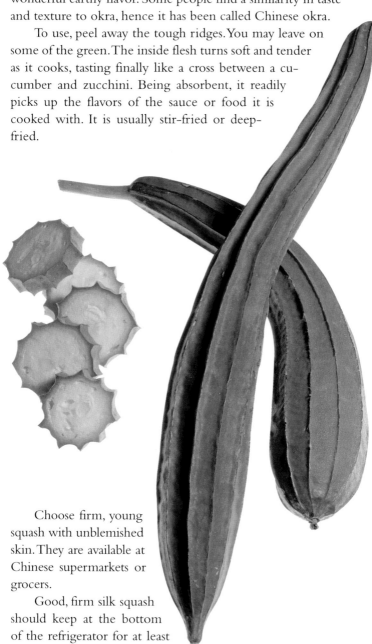

Choose firm, young squash with unblemished skin. They are available at Chinese supermarkets or grocers.

Good, firm silk squash should keep at the bottom of the refrigerator for at least 1 week.

SNOW PEAS
(Pisum sativum var. macrocarpon)

These delicacies are the early or spring variety of the common green pea, and are also known as **mange tout** or **sugar peas**. Native to the Middle East, peas were introduced into China by the Europeans, hence their literal Chinese name "Holland Peas." I would guess that the name snow peas comes from their being picked while some snow was still on the

ground, as is the case with the naming of red-in-the-snow cabbage (see page 14). The type available in the West is slightly larger than that found in China.

Many people who don't particularly enjoy eating green peas in general find snow peas delicious—no doubt because the younger peas are sweeter and less starchy. Many enjoy eating snow peas raw, which just shows that their tender, sweet crispiness needs little cooking. Thus, they are perfect for quick stir-fry dishes using a touch of oil, garlic, and ginger, or in combination with seasoned poultry or meat.

Look for pods that are firm and that have very small peas, which means they are tender and young.

Snow peas are readily available at supermarkets, and should be eaten as quickly as possible. However, they will keep for at least 3 days in the vegetable crisper of the refrigerator.

NOTES:

• String snow peas at their ends before using.

• To prepare, wash well, then remove the tops and tails. The whole pod with the peas inside should be cooked—hence their French name *mange tout*.

TARO

(Colocasia esculenta)

Taro root (actually a rhizome) is a venerable food that has been cultivated for a long time. It was used in China and Southeast Asia as a starch long before rice. Taros vary in shape, but they are roughly spherical, ranging from the size of a tennis ball to about 9 inches (42 cm) in diameter and often covered with a rough skin and brownish hairs. They are starchy with a sweet flavor and doughy texture, and are sometimes used as a source for flour. Taros have a whitish flesh, are sometimes streaked with purple, and can be cooked like potatoes. They are often combined with meats in braised dishes. Some taro varieties have edible leaves that may be prepared in the same way as mustard or turnip greens.

Taro is versatile enough to be used in desserts and as a paste for dim sum; it may also be deep-fried. Taro forms the basis of the Hawaiian poi, a cooked and fermented paste. Taros must be peeled before using—the corm, or fleshy, bulb-like base, is the edible part.

Buy firm-looking taros that are well-proportioned and without bruises. Store in a cool place (as you would store potatoes or onions), but use within the week.

WATER CHESTNUTS
(ELEOCHARIS DULCIS)

There are many water vegetables cultivated and eaten in China. The land is tiered by rice fields, and the cultivation of aquatic vegetables has been a natural development. It's because the vegetables are sometimes rotated with the rice crop or are grown alongside the rice that the fresh ones are often muddy. Most of these vegetables are grown in tropical or semitropical areas, as they require a long summer to develop. Authentic Chinese water chestnuts do not actually belong to the chestnut family at all but are part of this water vegetable family.

They are mahogany colored and shaped like a chestnut with papery layers attached to the skin that come to a tufted point in the center. They grow a perennial reed-like plant, with long, thick, hollow leaves over 2 feet (.6 m) high. They are a sweet, white, crunchy, and juicy vegetable that can be eaten raw as well as cooked.

Water chestnuts have been eaten in China for centuries. They are a popular snack either boiled in their skins or peeled and simmered in rock sugar. They need only light cooking and are often chopped or sliced and added to cooked dishes. They are also the source of water chestnut flour or powder, which is used to thicken sauces or to coat food. Another water vegetable that is also sometimes known as water chestnut is the two-horned water caltrop, which has a shiny black skin, but this is rarely available in the West.

Fresh water chestnuts can be obtained from Chinese markets or some supermarkets. Look for those with a firm, hard texture. The skin should be tight and taut, not wrinkled. If they are mushy, they are too old. Feel them all over for soft, rotten spots.

If you peel them in advance, cover them with cold water to prevent browning and store them in the refrigerator. Unpeeled and put in a paper bag in the refrigerator, they will keep for up to 2 weeks. They must be peeled before eating.

WATER SPINACH
(IPOMOEA AQUATICA)

Water spinach is widely grown throughout Asia, often escaping cultivation and growing wild on muddy river banks. It has no relationship to ordinary spinach. The leaves and tender stems are delicate and require little cooking. The pleasant, mild, sweet flavor and slightly slippery texture of the leaves when cooked contrast nicely with the crispness of the stems. Although water spinach is commonly green, there is a white-stemmed variety that is even more tender.

Like many water vegetables, the leaves are rich in vitamins and minerals. They are usually cooked as we do our familiar spinach: blanched, stir-fried, used in soup, and combined with meats. Look for the freshest looking leaves.

Like most leafy vegetables, they begin to wilt as soon as they are picked. However, they will keep for at least 2 days in the bottom part of your refrigerator.

WINTER MELON
(BENINCASA HISPIDA)

An ancient food of China, its name is a bit misleading. While these melons (which are really members of the squash family) do have a white coating that looks like a light dust of snow, they are harvested in the summer, then consumed during the winter months.

Being 1 to 2 feet (.3 to .6 m) in diameter, they look like oversized pale pumpkins. The edible core of the melon is soft and white with a subtle, sweet, mild flavor. It is most famous in winter melon soup, a spectacular dish for which the melon is carved to form a bowl. Melon pieces and a number of special ingredients are placed in a richly flavored broth and steamed in the melon itself. The entire ensemble is then served in the melon bowl.

Winter melons may be purchased whole or cut up. This is a most interesting vegetable and worth a taste.

Whole melons will keep for months in a cool, dry place. However, melon pieces should be used immediately.

INGREDIENTS

BEAN CURD

Bean curd, which is also known by its Chinese name, ***doufu***, or by its Japanese name, **tofu,** has played an important part in Chinese cookery since it originated, during the Han Dynasty (206 BC–AD 220). It became known as "meat without bones" because it is highly nutritious, rich in protein, and works well with other foods. It is also low in saturated fats and cholesterol, easy to digest, and inexpensive. Bean curd has a distinctive smooth, light, almost creamy texture but a bland taste. However, it is extremely versatile and lends itself to all types of cooking.

soft or silken bean curd

It is made from yellow soybeans that are soaked, ground, mixed with water, and then cooked briefly before being solidified. It is usually sold in two forms: in firm, small blocks or in a soft custard-like form, but it is also available in several dried forms and in a fermented version. The soft bean curd (sometimes called silken tofu) is used for soups and other dishes, while the solid type is used for stir-frying, braising, and deep-frying. Solid bean curd blocks are white in color and are packed in water in plastic containers.

If possible, purchase bean curd fresh from a Chinese market or grocer. While the commercial forms of bean curd available in supermarkets and health food stores are nutritious, they are ordinarily without the subtle flavor prized by bean curd lovers in China.

Once opened, the package of fresh bean curd may be kept in the refrigerator for up to 5 days,

firm bean curd

provided the covering water is changed daily. It is best to use the bean curd within 2 or 3 days of purchase.

NOTES:

- To use solid bean curd, cut the amount required by the recipe into cubes or shreds. Use a sharp knife and cut with care because the bean curd is fragile. It also needs to be cooked gently, as too much stirring can cause it to disintegrate. This does not, however, affect its nutritional value.

- Deep-frying bean curd transforms its texture into a sponge-like web, allowing the bean curd to absorb flavors when it is cooked for a second time with sauce.

Red, Chile, and Regular
Fermented Bean Curd

This is a cheese-like form of bean curd preserved in rice wine, in brine with rice wine, or in chiles and condiments. It is sold in glass jars at Chinese markets or grocers. It is very popular in China, where it is eaten by itself with rice or rice porridge, used as an ingredient in cooking, or featured as a seasoning. A little bit of it adds zest to any vegetable dish. Once it begins to cook, it produces a fragrant aroma that enriches the vegetables. Used in braised meat dishes, it blends with the sauce to give it an extraordinary aromatic taste and flavor.

It comes in several forms: the red fermented bean curd has been cured in a brine with fermented red rice (flavored with annatto seeds added to rice wine lees), Shaoxing rice wine, and sometimes crushed dried chile peppers; the regular variety is made with just rice wine. You can only find these preparations of bean curd at Chinese markets or grocers.

Many of the Hong Kong brand labels are good and recommended, as are the brands from China and Taiwan. It is

best to try several to find the one that fits your particular taste; they are extremely inexpensive. Some have a stronger wine taste, while others are salty and more briny in flavor.

Once the jar has been opened, fermented bean curd will keep indefinitely if resealed and refrigerated.

Pressed Seasoned Bean Curd

When water is extracted from fresh bean curd cakes by pressing them with a weight, the bean curd becomes firm and compact. Simmered in water with soy sauce, star anise, and sugar, the pressed bean curd acquires a smooth, resilient texture that is quite unusual. Cut into small pieces, it can be stir- fried with meat or vegetables; when cut into larger pieces it can be simmered. It is wonderful used in purely vegetarian dishes. For vegetarian dishes, simply brush the bean curd cakes with oil and grill them. Add them instead of meat to vegetables for a tasty main course. In China, pressed seasoned bean curd is a popular offering at many food stalls.

It can be found at Chinese grocers and supermarkets, usually in the refrigerated sections. Locally made Chinese brands tend to be quite good.

Pressed seasoned bean curd is often vacuum-packed, and as such it should keep in the refrigerator for at least 1 week. Once opened it should be used within 2 or 3 days.

BEAN SAUCE

Bean sauce, yellow bean sauce, brown bean sauce, bean paste, and **soybean condiment** are variations on a seasoning made from fermented soybeans that is one of the oldest forms of food flavoring in China. Before 200 BC, the Chinese used salted and fermented soybeans and

another type of thin, salty sauce, which were the precursors of the bean sauce of today, which is made from yellow or black dried soybeans that have been partially decomposed by adding a mold culture. Then the beans are salted, dried, or mixed with brine. This thick, spicy, aromatic sauce is mixed with yellow beans, flour, and salt, and fermented. There are two forms: whole beans in a thick sauce, and mashed or puréed beans (sold as crushed or yellow bean sauce). Depending on the recipe, one or the other is used. They are both strongly flavored and salty.

If labeled plain "bean sauce," it is likely made of whole beans. This is the preferred sauce, as it is rounder in flavor and has more of a textural bite. Often the ground version is very salty. In China, this is often purchased from local food shops that prepare the sauces according to favorite local recipes. People purchase what they need from large jars. Many of the versions available in cans or jars from China (Pearl River Bridge brand) or Hong Kong are quite good, especially the Koon Chun Sauce Factory's Bean Sauce.

If you buy the sauce in a can, transfer it to a glass jar. It will keep indefinitely in the refrigerator.

NOTE:

Bean sauce is a good foundation for making a favorite sauce: combine it with hoisin sauce (see page 74) and your favorite chile bean sauce (see page 55).

BEAN THREAD NOODLES

Also called **transparent** or **cellophane noodles,** these are not made from a grain flour but from ground mung beans, which are also the source of the more familiar bean sprouts. Freshly made ones can sometimes be seen on lines in China, fluttering in the breeze like long thread-like fabric. They are available dried, and are very fine and white. They're easy to recognize in their neat, plastic-wrapped bundles, and are stocked by most Chinese markets and some supermarkets. There are only a few brands available, and all are recommended. They come in packages from 1 ounce to 1 pound (about 28 to 454 g). I recommend the smaller 1- or 2-ounce (about 28- to 56-g) packages, as these are easier to handle and to measure. The ones most widely available are from China and are quite inexpensive.

Bean thread noodles are never served on their own but are added to soups or braised dishes or are deep-fried and used as a garnish. Once they are soaked they become soft and slippery, springy and translucent. Because they are a vegetable product, they are popular in vegetarian dishes. When fried, they puff up immediately and become very white and crispy, making a light, airy bed for stir-fried dishes.

If stored in a dry place, they will last indefinitely.

NOTE:

The noodles should be soaked in hot water rather than boiled for about 5 minutes before use. As they are rather long, you might find it easier to cut them into shorter lengths after soaking. If you are frying them, omit the soaking, but make sure to separate them first. A good technique for separating the strands is to put them into a large paper bag before pulling them apart; this stops them from flying all over the place.

BIRD'S NEST

A truly exotic food, bird's nest is one of the most sought-after delicacies of China. Historically, it was most popular in southern China, though served in other parts of China also. But it is now much sought after in affluent Hong Kong and Taiwan,

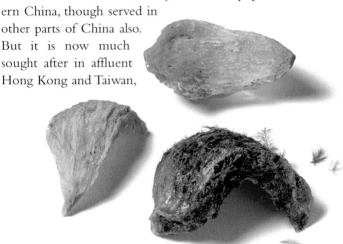

as well as throughout Southeast Asia. It is literally a bird's nest made with the regurgitated spittle of the *Collacallia*, a breed of swallow, from the east Asian tropics. Their nests are found in large caverns where workers climb on long bamboo scaffolding to retrieve them.

The gelatinous spittle of the nest is believed to possess powerful medicinal and youth-restoring virtues. Bird's nest is also said to be good for one's complexion and is prescribed for convalescing patients. There are shops in Hong Kong and Taiwan specializing in this delicacy, which comes in various grades. The best ones are the "white nests" and "pink or blood nests," which are expensive and are usually sold pre-cleaned (that is, feathers are hand-plucked from the nests). Bird's nest must be soaked before using. The result is a flavorless, soft, crunchy jelly that relies for flavor on savory or sweet sauces or broths. It is also used in extravagant stuffings.

Buy the best quality your budget can afford. This is by no means an ordinary household food. Beginners will need some expert guidance in gaining an appreciation of the virtues of this delicacy.

Because it is dried, it will keep in a dry place indefinitely.

NOTE:

To use, soak 8 or 9 hours or overnight in cold water. Simmer it for 20 minutes in plain water. Rinse again in cold water and squeeze dry before proceeding with the recipe.

BLACK BEANS

These small black soybeans, also known as **salted black beans** or **fermented black beans**, are preserved by being cooked and fermented with salt and spices, resulting in pungent, soft beans. They have a distinctive, salty taste and a pleasantly rich aroma and are often used as a seasoning, usually in conjunction with garlic, fresh ginger, or chiles. They are among the most popular flavors of southern China, but they are used less in other parts of China. Black beans are especially good in steamed, braised, and stir-fried dishes, imparting a rich flavor to every dish. They should not be confused with the dried black beans used in Western cooking.

They are readily available in the West in supermarkets. Although you can find them in cans marked "black bean sauce," I would avoid these. Instead, buy the ones that come packed in plastic bags. The best packaged variety is the Pearl River Bridge brand, labeled "Yang Jiang Preserved Beans (with Ginger)" from southern China. This brand has a rich, aromatic flavor that is inviting and assertive at the same time.

The beans will keep indefinitely if stored in the refrigerator or in a cool place. Take the beans from the package and transfer them to a clean, covered jar. Store away from light and heat.

NOTES:

• Depending on the recipe, the black beans should be *lightly* chopped or crushed to release their tangy aromas.

• Although some recipes say to rinse them before using, I find this unnecessary, as the salt adds to the flavor of the dish without overpowering the other flavors.

CHILE BEAN SAUCE OR PASTE

Chile peppers, both sweet and hot, were introduced into China scarcely one hundred years ago. Their popularity was immediate and, along with the tomato, they transformed Chinese cooking. There are many varieties of chile sauces and pastes, but the basic paste or sauce (also known as **chile paste with garlic** or **Sichuan chile sauce**) includes ground chiles, oil, salt, and garlic fermented into a rich paste that ranges in taste from mild to very hot. Chinese cooks will also mix into the basic version such ingredients as ground soybeans, black beans, ginger, preserved vegetables, and other condiments. In the so-called "hot bean pastes" soybeans predominate. Every chef in every region of China has his or her own special recipe for chile paste.

The brand you buy will greatly influence the taste of the dish that calls for this sauce. Unfortunately, none of the labels indicates whether the sauce is hot or mild. However, one of the best is the Lan Chi brand from Taiwan. It is a high-quality sauce that is well balanced with seasonings. There are many good brands from China, but, unfortunately, their availability is rather spotty; they should be purchased whenever they are available, especially the ones from Sichuan province. Brands like Amoy from Hong Kong tend to be of high quality and are generally milder, but there are a few very hot ones. It is best to try a few and decide what suits your palate. I would avoid many of the Singapore brands, which vary from bland to very hot without any balancing seasonings.

Be sure to seal the jar tightly after use and store in the refrigerator, where it will keep indefinitely.

NOTES:

- When using a chile bean sauce or paste for the first time, temper your usage until you are familiar with the flavor, then adjust the amount of sauce according to your taste.

- Combine chile bean sauce with other sauces, such as soy sauce (see page 98) or Shaoxing rice wine (see page 93), to create your own personal flavors.

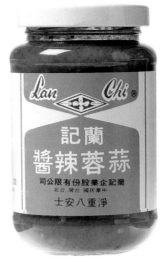

- Amoy makes a chile sauce (really, chile oil) that is used mainly as a dipping sauce. It is a hot, reddish, thin sauce made without any added beans and should not be confused with the thicker, more complex chile bean paste or sauce.

CHILE OIL OR DIPPING SAUCE

Chile oil is used extensively in Chinese cooking. It is sometimes used as a dipping condiment as well as a seasoning. Made from crushed dried chiles or small whole chiles, depending on the flavor you are seeking, it is used to impart a sharp, hot flavor to cooked dishes. However, chile oil is too dramatic to be used directly as the sole cooking oil; it is best combined with other, milder oils.

Because many store-bought versions can easily go rancid, it is better to make your own (see recipe on page 139). The Chinese and Taiwanese versions of commercially made chile oil are never as hot as the chile oils from Thailand and Malaysia. Of course, just as chiles vary in strength and flavor, so do the oils made with them. You can purchase chile oil from Chinese markets.

Once bought or made, chile oil should be stored in a tightly sealed glass jar in a cool, dark place. It will keep for months.

DRIED RED CHILES

Dried red chiles are used extensively in some regions of China. Drying is done for practical purposes—so that chiles are always available. In the southwest region of Sichuan province and in Hunan, China, one may see the long strings of dried red chiles hanging in kitchens of homes and restaurants. The drying process concentrates the power of the chile and adds vigor and complexity to spicy dishes. Chiles are often combined with other ingredients, such as peppercorns and garlic, to make a rather fiery concoction.

Look for dried chiles with a bright red color; they should have a pungent aroma. Dried chiles will keep indefinitely in a tightly covered jar in a cool place.

NOTE:

Larger dried chiles tend to be milder than the smaller ones. They are useful for making chile oil (see page 56, and recipe on page 139). They are most suited for use in stir-fried dishes; split and chopped, they are excellent in sauces and for braising. They are normally left whole or cut in half lengthwise with the seeds left in or finely ground, depending on your taste. Remember that leaving in the seeds increases the intensity, or hotness, of the chiles.

CINNAMON BARK
(CINNAMOMUM ZEYLANICUM, C. CASSIA)

Also known as **Chinese cinnamon** or **cassia,** cinnamon is produced in China exclusively from the bark of a type of laurel tree. It is one of the most ancient and widely known spices in the world. It was used in Egypt around 3000 BC, mentioned in Exodus (1700 BC), and already popular in China by 1000 BC.

In Chinese cuisine, its aromatic virtues are exploited particularly well in braised dishes. Cinnamon sticks (curled, paper-thin strips) have a concentrated and assertive spiciness that is preferred in recipes that involve robust flavors. The famous five-spice powder would be terribly lacking without its cinnamon element.

Look for thin, rolled cinnamon sticks or bark in Chinese markets or grocers. They are usually found in plastic bags and are inexpensive and very fresh. If you find the bark, look for firm, aromatic pieces. Avoid packages that are broken up into small bits. Ground cinnamon is not a satisfactory substitute for cinnamon bark or sticks.

Store cinnamon sticks or bark in a tightly sealed jar to preserve their aroma and flavor.

NOTE:

Cassia, which is more strongly scented than true cinnamon, is derived from the bark of a different type of laurel tree than cinnamon is. Most of the so-called cinnamon sold in America is actually cassia. True cinnamon is tan in color; cassia is a darker reddish brown.

This ingredient is also known as **dried tangerine peel** or **dried orange peel.**

Until this century, fresh fruits were relatively expensive and, therefore, an infrequent part of the diet of most people. Orange and tangerine peels, which were tossed out by most, were highly valued by the less fortunate. The concentrated essence of these golden fruits served to enliven many prosaic dishes and to recall to people the warm glow of summertime. In

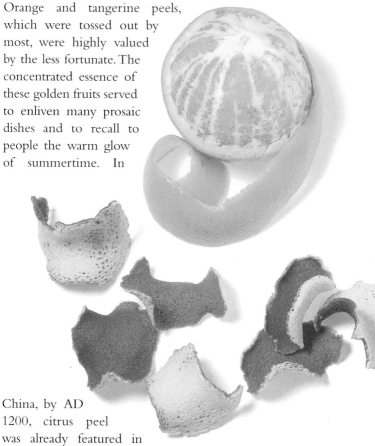

China, by AD 1200, citrus peel was already featured in many dishes. In a single orange-growing area as many as eighty thousand pounds of citrus peel were produced each year.

As with many acidic foods, the peels have been used as a medicine in China for centuries. Today, they serve mainly as a seasoning ingredient. The most cherished are the peels of Chinese tangerines, which have a rich aroma and flavor. Citrus peels are often used as additives in braised or simmered dishes, their fruity essence suffusing the entire dish. Occasionally, the peels are used in "master sauces," providing them with a contrasting flavor dimension. More rarely, they are used in stir-fry dishes.

Dried citrus peel can be bought in Asian or Chinese grocery stores or can be easily made at home.

Stored in an airtight jar, the dried peel will last for months or years. When you are ready to use the peel, rehydrate it in a bowl of warm water for 20 minutes, or until it is soft. It can also be rehydrated in Shaoxing rice wine (see page 93). The hydrating wine can then be used in the dishes themselves.

NOTE:

To make citrus peel at home, wash and rinse the fruit well. Use a good vegetable peeler to carefully peel the skin off the fruit. Then use a sharp knife to carefully separate the white pith from the peel. Dry the peel on a rack in a warm place until it is hard, or place on a tray in direct sunlight. When the peels are dried, store as instructed above. These peels improve with age.

CLOUD EARS

These edible fungi are also known as **tree ears, black fungus, black tree fungus, *mu-er*, wood ear,** and **wood fungus**. As the names indicate, they grow on trees, deriving the growth chemicals they lack from the wood of either live or decaying trees. They have been used in Chinese cooking since the sixth century AD and have always been highly regarded for their supposed medicinal value, particularly as purifiers of the blood. Most of these mushrooms have little or no discernible taste on their own. Rather, they readily take on the flavors of the foods with which they are cooked, flavors they mysteriously help to bring out. In addition, their distinctive and pleasing texture adds to the enjoyment of other ingredients.

There are two main types and sizes of these mushrooms. The small, black, dried, flaky variety are known as cloud ears because when soaked, they puff up like fleecy little clouds. The larger variety of tree fungi have a slightly tough but still pleasant crunchy texture.

You can find them wrapped in plastic or cellophane bags

at Chinese markets. Many are from China and are repackaged by the grocer who is selling them. They should be hard and dry. They keep indefinitely in a jar stored in a cool dry place.

NOTE:

To prepare cloud ears or wood ears, soak them in hot water for about 15 minutes, or until they are soft. They should then be rinsed several times to remove any sand. Trim the hard stems of the wood ears before using. Once soaked, they will swell up to four or five times their size.

CORN OIL

Corn oil is light and mostly polyunsaturated, and has a high burning temperature. Being thus similar to peanut oil (see page 79), it is an adequate substitute for Chinese stir-frying and deep-frying. Store in a cool, dry place, away from light.

CURRY PASTE OR POWDER

Curry is derived from the leaves of a plant native to southwest Asia. Like "chutney," "curry" does not mean one particular flavor. Curry powders and pastes are in fact made up of different combinations of spices and seasonings. In India, most noted for its curries, curry is a generic term for a great number of possible sauces.

All curries are pungent, but they range in taste from hot to mild. There are no all-purpose curry powders. In the West, most curry powders are made up mainly of turmeric, and the presence of other spices is determined more by economic than culinary standards.

Curries were brought to southern China centuries ago by Chinese merchants returning from India. Because they are pungent, they never really caught on. Their strength is perceived as an interference with the enjoyment of the flavors of fresh foods. Curries are used in China—but sparingly.

Many of the brands from India have an authentic taste. Buy the Madras curry paste or powder variety, which has a rich, spicy, and complex taste that is excellent for Chinese dishes.

Curry paste or powder will keep indefinitely in the refrigerator.

NOTE:

Do not confuse Indian curry paste (described above) with Thai curry paste, which is quite different.

dried scallops

DRIED SEAFOOD

By the time of the Sung Dynasty (AD 960–1289), fish and shellfish had become so popular in Chinese cuisine that poets began to wax lyrical over them, dropping their conceits concerning the previous favorite, chicken, which disappeared as a poetic theme. This emergence of seafood and fish reflected a cultural shift to southern China, where fish and shellfish had long been favorites and where there are thousands of species, both wild and pond reared.

Before the age of refrigeration and rapid transport of goods, drying, salting, and pickling were the only ways to preserve foods for any length of time. With these methods, the food retains much of its nutritional value and, as such, becomes a year-round part of the diet. However, the drawback is that flavors and aromas become concentrated and often powerful. The remedy is to use the foods sparingly, as a condiment or flavoring ingredient, knowing that in the cooking process the wilder flavors are usually domesticated.

Fish are the most prevalent dried seafood in China. All types and sizes are thus preserved, often in a semimoist state that is a great favorite with southern Chinese. The dried fish are cut up and fried or steamed, sometimes alone but more often in combination with other foods. Today, we have fresh fish available to us, but the dried versions still retain their place in the cuisine as providers of a special taste and aroma.

Other dried seafood include abalone, squid, scallops, jellyfish, and shrimp (prawns).

There are many varieties of dried fish and shellfish. The

quality is simply based on price. The more exotic and desirable varieties cost more than the lesser and more abundant ones. Some dried fish also come packed in oil and are very good; look for the brands from Hong Kong or China. These tend to all be of high quality and quite good.

Dried fish will keep indefinitely when simply dried or when kept in oil. Store in a cool, dry place, away from light.

NOTE:

Soak dried fish or shellfish in warm water for 30 minutes. When it has softened, remove any bones and chop. Some dried seafood, like abalone and squid, needs to be soaked for up to 24 hours before using.

dried oysters

dried abalone

Dried shrimp (prawns) are used as a seasoning to perk up fried rice and other dishes. They give an added dimension to soups and stuffings. They are essentially made of small peeled shrimp dehydrated by the sun or air-dried.

When cooked, the dried shrimp add a delicate taste to sauces; cooking moderates the shrimp's strong odors.

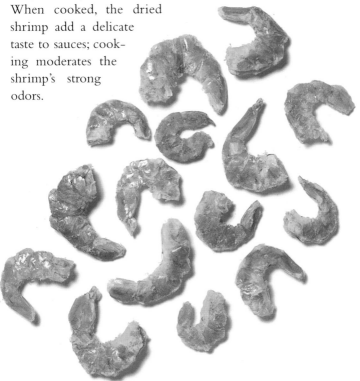

Look for the brands with the brightest orange-pink color. Avoid grayish ones, which may be old. Dried shrimp are sold in packages and may be found in Chinese grocers or markets.

Dried shrimp will keep indefinitely if sealed in a glass container and kept in the refrigerator. They can also be kept in the freezer if well wrapped, or, if you plan to use them within a month's time, they may be stored in a cool, dry place.

NOTE:

Soak them in warm water or Shaoxing rice wine (see page 93) or steam them to soften them before using. The soaking liquid may be used in the dish.

DRIED SHRIMP ROE

Dried shrimp (prawn) roe are minuscule and orange-red. Not to be confused with caviar, they are dried and salted, which transforms them into tiny, red, hard grains. Like other dried seafood used in Chinese cooking, they have a strong odor and flavor. They are usually sprinkled sparingly over soups, vegetable dishes, egg dishes, or dumplings. Such a garnish highlights by contrast the flavors of other foods.

This is a rather rare and expensive ingredient found on occasion at some Chinese grocers. It should be stored in a glass jar and kept in the refrigerator.

DUCK EGGS

Preserved Duck Eggs

These are fresh duck eggs preserved in a brine mixture. The brine seeps into the shell and the whites become salty; the yolks become firm and orange-colored and have a rich flavor and taste. These eggs are used in Chinese moon cakes (pastries filled with sweet bean paste) and other salty pastries,

thousand-year-old eggs

as well as in savory steamed dishes. They can also be hard-boiled and eaten as snacks or appetizers. The eggs must be well-rinsed before using. Unopened eggs can be kept for many months.

Thousand-Year-Old Eggs

These are duck eggs which have been preserved in a mixture of fine ash, clay, and salt. The whites turn a translucent black and the yolks turn a grayish-green. They are used in pastries and as appetizers, usually with pickled ginger. Rinse them thoroughly before using. Unopened eggs can be kept for many months.

EGG NOODLES AND WHEAT NOODLES

It has been said that pasta noodles started in northern China around 100 BC. However, noodles are rarely made in the home, as commercial noodle-making is such an ancient craft. It is common to find fresh noodles of all types available throughout China and in many parts of the world where there is a substantial Chinese-speaking community. They are an important element of the Chinese diet.

There are many types of noodles. An important one is the egg noodle, which is made from wheat flour and egg, a bit like Italian pasta. Most common are the thin, round strands that are sold fresh or dried. Occasionally, they are flavored with fish or shrimp (prawns) to give them additional flavors. They tend to be yellowish in color and are used in stir-fried dishes as well as in soups. Wheat noodles have no eggs; they are made from wheat flour, water, and salt, and are whiter in color. They are also available fresh or dried. The dried noodles are made from hard or soft wheat flour and water. Like egg noodles, they are used in soups as well as in stir-fried dishes.

Although many types of fresh noodles are now available in supermarkets, they tend to be more starchy than Chinese-made noodles. Fresh egg or wheat noodles available in Chinese markets or grocers are usually the best. However, many of the brands of dried noodles from either China or Hong Kong are also of high quality and are recommended. They are also quite inexpensive.

Dried noodles keep indefinitely, while fresh noodles will keep in the bottom part of your refrigerator for only 2 or 3 days. Fresh noodles freeze well.

egg noodles

Notes:

- If you are using fresh noodles, immerse them in a pot of boiling water and cook them for 3 to 5 minutes, or until you find their texture done to your taste. If you are using dried noodles, either cook them according to the instruc-

tions on the package, or cook them in salted boiling water for 4 to 5 minutes. Drain and serve.

- It is best to give the fresh noodles a quick rinse before stir-frying them or putting them in soups.

wheat noodles

- Frozen fresh noodles should be thawed thoroughly before blanching in simmering salted water.

- If you are cooking noodles ahead of time or before stir-frying them, toss the cooked and drained noodles in 2 tea-

spoons (10 ml) of sesame oil and put them into a bowl. Cover this with plastic wrap and refrigerate. The cooked noodles will remain usable for about 2 hours.

FISH SAUCE

Fish sauces, the product of salted and fermented fish, have long been a staple in Southeast Asia and are used like soy sauce there. They are used occasionally in southern China, perhaps brought back by Chinese returning from Southeast Asia. A fish sauce is usually a clear, brownish, salty liquid that is rich in protein. The sauces, in fact, were originally concocted as a means of preserving fish protein. Also known as **fish gravy,** *nước mâm* in Vietnam or *nam pla* in Thailand, fish sauce has a strong odor and a taste to match. Cooking it or mixing it with other ingredients, however, diminishes the

"fishy" flavor and allows the sauce to add a special richness, fragrance, and quality to dishes. It is also used as a dipping sauce, usually combined with other ingredients to mitigate its strong flavors.

It is said that the best brands come from Vietnam and Thailand. However, Vietnamese brands are not always readily available. Fortunately, many of the Thai brands can easily be found in Chinese markets or grocers. Viet Huong's "Three Crab Brand Fish Sauce" and Flying Lion's "Phy Quoc," both from Thailand, are highly recom- mended.

Fish sauces in bottles will keep indefinitely. Store them in a cool, dry place.

FIVE-SPICE POWDER

This ancient spice formula harmonizes star anise, Sichuan peppercorn, fennel, clove, and cinnamon or the stronger cassia. But why stop at five spices? The answer perhaps lies not in cookery but in cosmology. In ancient Chinese lore, the universe is composed of five elements: wood, metal, water, fire, and earth. Some combinations of these were believed to be harmonious, others disharmonious, so that care had to be taken in mixing them together. This fivefold categorization was carried over into daily life. Thus, just as the elements of the universe had to be carefully balanced, so, too, did the elements of civil life have to be harmonized. In the preparation of food especially, the proper fivefold relationships had to be created and maintained. One result was five-spice powder, which traditionally had powerful medicinal as well as culinary potency. On the other hand, it might have been just an accidental concatenation that worked to perfection.

Whatever its provenance, this spice is pungent, fragrant, hot, mild, and slightly sweet—all at once. Its distinct fragrance and unique flavor turn the most prosaic dish into something special.

Spices are always better freshly ground. There are no "brand name" five-spice powders, and given our new cosmology, sometimes there are more or fewer than five spices in the package. The mixture is sold in good Chinese supermarkets and Asian specialty shops and comes in plastic bags or small glass jars. You should experiment with a number of them to find the one that suits your taste. They are all inexpensive.

Store in a tightly closed glass jar in a cool, dry place.

NOTES:

• Five-spice powder is wonderful mixed with salt for a dipping condiment.

• It should be used in small quantities, as a little goes a long way.

• Try it with grilled meats.

HOISIN SAUCE

Hoisin sauce is part of the bean sauce family. It is a rich, thick, brownish red sauce that is made from soybean paste, garlic, vinegar, sugar, spices, and other flavorings. It is at once sweet and spicy. The texture ranges from creamy thick to thin. It is

used in China as a condiment and as a glaze for roasted meats. In the West, it is often used as a sauce (mixed with sesame oil) for Peking duck instead of the traditional bean sauce. Hoisin sauce is sold in cans and jars. (It is sometimes also called barbecue sauce with hoisin sauce; however, check carefully, as there are barbecue sauces available that are quite different from hoisin sauce.)

The best hoisin sauce comes from China under

the brand name of Pearl River Bridge. Another good one from China is under the Ma Ling label. Other good brands are from Hong Kong, under the Amoy and Koon Chun Sauce Factory's label. Chee Hou Sauce is a slightly stronger version of hoisin sauce and can be used as a substitute for hoisin sauce.

LILY BUDS
(HEMEROCALLIS SPP.)

Also known as **tiger lily buds, golden needles,** or **lily stems,** dried lily buds are the unopened flowers of a type of day lily. About 2 inches (5 cm) in length, they have a slightly furry texture and an earthy fragrance. The buds serve well as an ingredient in *muxi* (*mu shu*), a stir-fried pork dish with cloud ear mushrooms (see page 60), and hot and sour soup, providing a vegetable-like texture (but no real flavor) to dishes.

Buy lily buds that are bright golden yellow in color. Avoid dark, brittle ones, as they are too old. They're available in plastic or cellophane bags from Chinese grocers or supermarkets. They are very inexpensive.

Transfer the lily buds to a jar and store in a cool, dry place. They will keep indefinitely.

NOTE:
To use, soak the buds in hot water for about 20 minutes, or until soft. Cut off the hard ends and shred or cut in half according to the recipe directions.

CHINESE DRIED BLACK MUSHROOMS
(Lentinus edodes)

These "black" mushrooms actually range from light brown to dark brown in color. The most popular are the larger-sized, light brown ones with a highly cracked surface. These are, predictably, the most expensive ones. But all versions and grades of this mushroom add a most desirable flavor and aroma to Chinese recipes. It is interesting to note that these mushrooms grow on fallen, decaying trees; the Chinese have been gathering them for over a thou-sand years.

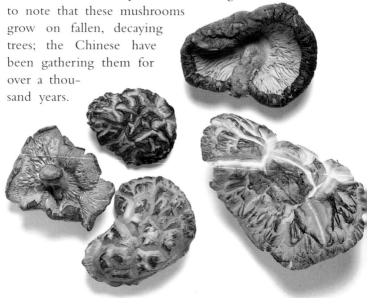

The Japanese cultivate them by growing them on the *shii* tree, hence the familiar fresh shiitake mushrooms.

The Chinese rarely eat these mushrooms fresh but prefer the dried version. The drying process concentrates their smoky flavors and robust taste and allows them to absorb sauces and spices, imparting to the mushrooms an even more succulent texture. This makes them most appropriate for use as seasonings, finely chopped and combined with meats, fish, or poultry.

So marvelous a treat must have medicinal properties, and sure enough, these dried black mushrooms are prescribed for respiratory and other problems. In Chinese markets that specialize in dried foods, you will find all grades and types of mushrooms heaped in large mounds, with the most expensive types elaborately boxed or wrapped in plastic, ready for use as food or medicine.

Depending on your budget, the lighter and more expensive grade is the best to buy. These should be reserved for special occasions. However, for normal, everyday fare, a moderately priced, good-quality mushroom is fine.

Keep them stored in an air-tight container. They will

keep indefinitely in a cool, dry place. If they are not to be used often, store them in the freezer.

NOTE:

To use, soak the mushrooms in a bowl of warm water for about 20 minutes, or until they are soft and pliable. Squeeze out the excess water and cut off and discard the woody stems. Only the caps are used. The soaking water can be saved and used in soups, as the water to make rice, and as a base for a vegetarian stock to add to sauces or braised dishes. Strain through a fine sieve to discard any sand or residue from the dried mushrooms.

OYSTER SAUCE

This very popular and versatile southern Chinese sauce is a thick, brown, richly flavored concoction that is one of the most ancient sauces in the culinary canon. Fresh oysters are boiled in large vats and then seasoned with soy sauce, salt, spices,

and seasonings and made into a viscous substance. The original version contained bits of dried fermented oysters, but these are no longer included.

The salty, "fishy" taste of oysters largely dissipates during the cooking process, but the sauce retains its rich and distinctive savory flavor, one that goes nicely with the preferred subtleties of southern Chinese cuisine. It is also used as a condiment or dipping sauce, diluted with a little oil, for vegetables, poultry, and meats.

It is usually sold in bottles and can be bought in Chinese markets and some supermarkets. Search out the most expensive ones; they tend to be less salty, have more flavor, and have less cornstarch added—their higher quality is worth the price. Cheaper oyster sauces tend to have MSG, as well as other additives, to make up for the lack of oysters used.

I have found two good brands from China and Hong Kong: one is Sa Cheng's "Oyster Flavored Sauce from China" and another is Hop Sing Lung's "Oyster Flavored Sauce," which is more available.

Oyster sauce is best kept in the refrigerator, where it will last indefinitely.

PEANUTS
(Arachis hypogaea)

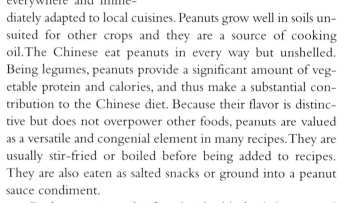

Peanuts (groundnuts) are a wonderfully successful transplant. Introduced by way of the Portuguese—from the New World to Manila to Macao to China and elsewhere in Asia—the peanut has been enthusiastically adopted everywhere and immediately adapted to local cuisines. Peanuts grow well in soils unsuited for other crops and they are a source of cooking oil. The Chinese eat peanuts in every way but unshelled. Being legumes, peanuts provide a significant amount of vegetable protein and calories, and thus make a substantial contribution to the Chinese diet. Because their flavor is distinctive but does not overpower other foods, peanuts are valued as a versatile and congenial element in many recipes. They are usually stir-fried or boiled before being added to recipes. They are also eaten as salted snacks or ground into a peanut sauce condiment.

Fresh peanuts can be found at health food shops, good

supermarkets, and Chinese markets. Make sure they are well-packaged so that they do not become rancid.

Store them in a glass jar in a cool, dry place.

NOTE:

The thin, red skins need to be removed before you use the nuts. To do this, simply immerse them in a pot of boiling water for about 2 minutes. Drain nuts and let them cool. The skins will come off easily. Stir-fry or roast the peanuts just before using.

PEANUT OIL

Soybeans and peanuts (groundnuts) are unique among the legumes in that they store oil instead of starch. This feature has long been exploited in China, where peanut oil has become the most popular cooking oil because of its mild, unobtrusive taste and because it heats to high temperatures without burning. It is thus perfect for stir-frying and deep-frying.

The semi-refined peanut oils in China are cold-pressed and retain the fragrance of fresh peanuts and a distinctive flavor preferred by many cooks. Some Asian supermarkets in the West stock the Chinese brands of semi-refined peanut oil from either Hong Kong or China. The Lion and Globe brand from Hong Kong is very good; however, the best brand (if you can get it) is the one with Chinese characters for "double happiness." It comes in a gold and red can and is well worth the search. If you cannot find the imported brands, use the best-quality local peanut oil from your supermarket instead, looking for semi-refined oil. It should be stored in a cool, dry place, away from light.

PLUM SAUCE

Plums have been grown in China since ancient times. The fresh fruits spoil quickly. In order to capture their juicy richness, the Chinese preserve them with ginger, chile, spices, vinegar, and sugar. The result is a sweet, tart, jam-like condiment that is used as a cooking ingredient in recipes that call for assertive flavors. It is a popular item in Chinese restaurants where it is sometimes used inauthentically with Beijing (or Peking) duck.

Some of the best brands are from Hong Kong. Especially recommended is the Koon Chun Sauce Factory's plum sauce. Brands from China are quite good, although they are harder to find and available occasionally.

If you purchase the sauce in a can, transfer it to a glass jar and keep in the refrigerator, where it will last indefinitely.

PRESERVED MUSTARD GREENS OR CABBAGE
(Brassica juncea)

Mustard greens are known in Chinese as "greens heart" because only the heart of the plant is eaten, that is, the stem, buds, and young leaf. They are unrelated to and quite unlike the mustard greens of the American south. These greens are a vital part of the Chinese diet, being rich in vitamins and minerals and easy to cultivate. As such, they are enjoyed year round, either fresh or preserved. The leaves are pickled with salt, water, vinegar, and sugar, making a true sweet-and-sour food that is used as a vegetable or as a flavoring ingredient, especially in soups. It can be served as a snack or in stir-fries with meats, poultry, or fish.

The best form of these preserved mustard greens can be found in large crocks in Chinese markets, which usually means it is locally made. The next best alternative is available in small crocks or cans, labelled "preserved vegetable," from Hong Kong, Taiwan, or China. All are recommended.

Remove from the crock or can and store in a glass jar. It will keep indefinitely in the refrigerator.

RICE

Rice is the staple food for half of the world's population. It was first cultivated in prehistoric times in either India or China. In southern China, the phrase *chi fan*, "to eat rice," also means simply, "to eat," while the word *fan,* "cooked rice," "cooked grains," also means simply "food." Rice is perhaps the most useful plant known to humans: it is the source not only of food, wine, and vinegar, but of straw used for fodder, thatch, sandals, and other commercial uses.

Among the virtues of rice as a food, beyond its unquestionable nutritional value, is its warm congeniality with so many other foods and with so many spices and seasonings. By changing the cooking time, rice can be made into baby food, porridge, and other nutritious dishes. Even the water that remains after the rice is cooked can be saved and made into a cooling drink. Rice flour, of course, serves myriad purposes. It is no wonder that there can be no true meal in most of Asia without a serving of rice. Many varieties of rice are available in any supermarket, and all varieties listed below can be found in Asian supermarkets or grocers. It should always be stored in a cool, dry place, and will keep for a very long time.

Long-Grain White Rice

The favored variety of rice in China is the white, long-grain type, which cooks up relatively dry into easily separated grains. Most brands of long-grain white rice available in supermarkets are highly recommended. Especially good is the fragrant Thai long-grain rice found in Asian grocers or supermarkets. Although the Chinese go through the ritual of washing it, rice purchased at supermarkets doesn't require this step.

The best method to cook long-grain white rice is this: first, always cover the rice with about 1 inch (2.5 cm) of water. (Many package recipes for rice call for too much water and result in a gluey mess.) Cook the rice in an uncovered pot at high heat until most of the water has evaporated—about 15 minutes. Then the heat should be turned very low, the pot covered, and the rice cooked slowly in the remaining steam. As a child I was always instructed never to peek into the rice pot during this stage or else precious steam would escape and the rice would not be cooked properly, thus bringing bad luck.

Short-Grain White Rice

Short-grain white rice is slightly stickier than long-grain white rice, making it easier to eat with chopsticks. This non-glutinous rice is more frequently eaten in Japan than in China, though it is useful for making rice porridge, a popular southern Chinese morning dish.

All the best brands are Japanese. Cook it the same way you would long-grain white rice, with slightly less water (covering the rice by about ¾ inch or 2 cm)

Black Rice

Long-grain black rice is popular in Indonesia and the Philippines. It looks like wild rice but has a higher gluten content and is sticky when cooked. It is often combined with coconut milk and sugar or used in other sweet desserts. It is

also ground into flour. Black rice should be soaked for about 2 hours before using.

Red Rice

Red rice (not pictured) is grown throughout Asia and is similar to brown rice in taste and flavor. Generally used by poor farmers in China, it is not a highly regarded grain. It is part of the glutinous rice family, and should be soaked for about 2 hours before cooking.

Fresh rice noodles are very popular in southern China, where they are widely known as **Sha He noodles**. The name *Sha He* derives from that of a small village outside of Guangzhou (Canton). The villagers proudly claim that their ancestors discovered the process of fresh noodle-making. (They have so far refrained from demanding royalties.)

Fresh rice, or *fen,* noodles are made from a mixture of

rice flour, wheat starch (not flour), and water. This "pasta" is steamed into large sheets and then, when cooked, is cut into noodles to be eaten immediately. Restaurants and street food stalls in southern Chinese cities specialize in offering this nutritious and tasty treat, most often serving the dish in a broth or sauce.

Dried rice noodles are made from a dough of finely ground rice flour and water. This pasta is then extruded into opaque white noodles of varying thickness and sizes. One of the most common types is rice stick noodles, which are flat and about the length of a chopstick. Deep-fried, they puff up instantly and become delicately crisp and light. Because they are absorbent and have little flavor of their own, they readily take on the taste and fragrance of the foods with which they are cooked. They are a basic and extremely versatile food.

All dried rice noodle brands can be recommended, especially the ones from China and Thailand. They come attractively wrapped in paper or cellophane, and are often tied with red ribbon. Fresh rice noodles can be found only in Chinese markets or grocers.

Dried rice noodles stored in a dry, cool place will last indefinitely. Fresh rice noodles are best eaten on the day they are purchased. They can be refrigerated for 2 days, but you should let them soften at room temperature before stir-frying or preparing them.

NOTE:

Rice noodles are very easy to use. Simply soak them in warm water for 20 minutes, or until they are soft. Drain them in a colander or sieve, and use, for example, in soups or stir-fries. Dried rice noodles are perfect for quick, easy cooking, as they take little time to soften and can be cooked with almost any vegetable, meat, fish, or seafood.

RICE PAPERS

Known in Vietnam as **bánh tráng**, rice papers are made from a mixture of rice flour, water, and salt. Rolled out by a machine to paper thinness, they are then dried on bamboo mats in the sun, giving them their beautiful cross-hatch imprint or pattern. They are available only in dry form: round or triangular sheets that are dry, semitransparent, thin, and hard. They are used extensively for wrapping Vietnamese spring rolls of pork and seafood, which are then fried and wrapped with crispy, fresh lettuce and herbs and finally dipped in a sweet-and-sour hot sauce. Chiefly identified with Vietnamese cooking, rice papers have also become quite popular and are often

used by restaurants in Hong Kong, Taiwan, and parts of southern China.

Available for purchase in many Chinese grocers and supermarkets, they come in packages of 50 to 100 sheets. They are very inexpensive and all brands are good, especially the ones from Vietnam and Thailand. Look for white rice papers and avoid the yellowish ones, which may be too old. Broken pieces in the package may also indicate age.

Store them in a dry, cool place. After use, wrap the remaining rice papers carefully in the package they came in. Put this in another plastic bag and seal well before storing.

Note:

Rice paper must be softened before use. Carefully dip 1 or 2 sheets of the rice paper in a warm sugar-water solution or in beer. Soak them until they are soft, 1 or 2 minutes. Using a sugar-water solution or beer will result in a golden, crispy-looking spring roll. Drain them on a linen towel before rolling.

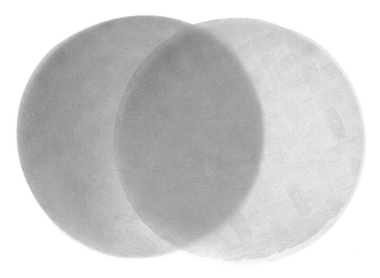

RICE VINEGARS

Vinegar is one of the oldest seasonings used in Asian cuisine; its name appears in documents from the twelfth century BC. Vinegars used in Asian cooking are usually made from fermented rice and grains such as wheat, millet, and sorghum. They should not be confused with Western wine vinegars, which are much more acidic and cannot serve as a substitute. Nor should rice vinegar be confused with Shaoxing rice wine (see page 93).

Stored at room temperature, rice vinegars will keep indefinitely. There are several types.

Black Rice Vinegar

Black rice vinegar is very dark in color with a rich but mild taste and an appealing depth of flavor. It is similar to

balsamic vinegar. It is usually made from glutinous rice, which imparts its mildness and taste. Really good black rice vinegar has a rich, impressive complexity of flavors and aromas. In northern Chinese dishes it is used for braised dishes, noodles, and sauces. Gold Blum's Chinkiang Vinegar from China is the best.

Red Rice Vinegar

Red rice vinegar is a clear, pale red vinegar. It has a delicate, tart, slightly sweet and salty taste and is usually used as a dipping sauce for seafood, or in shark's fin soup. Koon Chun brand from Hong Kong is best.

Sweet Rice Vinegar

This vinegar is brownish-black and thicker than plain rice vinegar. It looks a bit like dark soy sauce. It is processed

with sugar and star anise, and the result is an aromatic, caramel taste. Unlike other vinegars, it has very little tartness. It is used in large quantities for braised pork dishes. China's Pearl River brand is the best.

White Rice Vinegar

White rice vinegar is clear and mild in flavor. It has a faint taste of glutinous rice and is used for sweet-and-sour dishes. The Pearl River brand from China is best. Western cider vinegar can be substituted.

SESAME OIL

Native to India and one of the world's oldest spices, sesame seeds produce an aromatic oil that is golden or dark brown in color, thick, rich, and strong-flavored. This latter quality explains why it is not used as a cooking oil in China, but only for flavoring. Lighter, more subtly flavored oils are preferable for cooking.

Sesame oil is a wonderful aromatic addition to marinades, whether Chinese or otherwise.

Use it like walnut oil, adding a few drops to your salad dressing or dipping sauce.

The purest and best sesame oil is the Kadoya brand of Japan. It has a clean, fresh, aromatic flavor. Brands from China, Hong Kong, and Taiwan can be very good, although you can occasionally stumble upon a bottle that is rancid. This is due to storage and shipping time. Avoid any sesame oil that comes in plastic bottles, as the chances of it turning rancid are great. Store in a cool, dry place away from direct light.

SESAME PASTE

This rich, creamy, light brown paste is made from toasted sesame seeds. Sesame seeds were introduced into China over two thousand years ago. Chinese sesame paste is quite different from the Mediterranean tahini, whose seeds are raw when ground, producing a much lighter color and taste.

The Chinese use the paste in sauces and as an integral ingredient in both hot and cold dishes. Sesame paste is most popular in northern and western China. The hotter, wetter climate of eastern and southern China is uncongenial to the sesame plant.

I highly recommend all brands from China (especially Pearl River Bridge brand), Hong Kong, and Taiwan (Lan Chi brand), which are sold in jars at Chinese markets.

Kept in the refrigerator, sesame paste will last indefinitely.

NOTES:

- If the paste has separated in the jar, empty the contents into a blender or food processor and blend or process well. Always stir well before using.

- If you have a recipe that calls for sesame paste, and you can't locate some, use a smooth peanut (groundnut) butter instead.

SESAME SEEDS
(SESAMUM INDICUM)

The sesame plant is native to central Asia, Indonesia, or East Africa. It is cultivated today in the Middle East, Africa, China, and Japan. The seeds are highly valued, being rich in protein and in polyunsaturated oil. They are usually pressed into oils or made into pastes to serve as flavoring agents or in sauces. Seeds may be toasted and used as a garnish for savory foods, sweets, and breads. In China, there are sweeter varieties that are used in dessert soups. Toasted, they make a good snack food.

Purchase them untoasted in small plastic bags or in glass jars from supermarkets or Chinese grocers. Store them in a glass jar in a cool, dry place. They should last in-definitely, though some people prefer to freeze them to keep them from getting rancid. If you don't use them often, check the sesame seeds to make sure they are fresh. Toss them out if they have a rancid smell.

NOTE:

To toast sesame seeds, heat a frying pan or skillet until hot. Add the sesame seeds and stir occasionally. Watch them closely. When they begin to lightly brown, after about 3 to 5 minutes, stir them again and pour them onto a plate to cool. As an alternative, preheat the oven to 325°F (170°C). Spread the sesame seeds on a baking sheet. Roast them in the oven for about 10 to 15 minutes until they are nicely toasted and lightly browned. Allow them to cool and place in a glass jar until you are ready to use them.

Rice wine has been an integral part of Chinese cuisine for over two thousand years. At banquets and special feasts it is an essential element. (I should note that the Chinese know how to make wine from wheat, millet, and other grains.) About a thousand years ago, wines made from grapes were popular, but they eventually lost out to the ever popular rice wine. It is made from a blend of glutinous rice, millet, yeast, and spring water.

Shaoxing rice wine is China's most famous wine. It is known in Chinese as *hua tiao,* or "carved flower," from the name given to the pattern carved on the urns in which the wine is stored. The wine is kept in cellars until it matures, usually for ten years, although some have been

aged for as long as one hundred years. With its amber color, bouquet, and alcohol content, it resembles sherry. The wine is drunk warm or at room temperature, and is always consumed in the context of a meal.

Rice wine is an indispensable ingredient in many recipes, imparting a rich flavor and aroma to all sorts of dishes. It is also used in marinades and sauces.

If kept tightly corked at room temperature, it will last indefinitely.

NOTES:

- Do not confuse Shaoxing rice wine with Japanese sake, which is a Japanese version of rice wine and quite different. Nor should one confuse this wine with Chinese rice vinegars, which are vinegars, not wines.

- A good-quality, dry, pale sherry can be substituted but cannot equal its rich, mellow taste. Western grape wines are not adequate substitutes.

SHARK'S FIN

Although shark meat has been eaten for a long time, it is the fin that is an exotic delicacy of China, and one of the most expensive ingredients in Chinese cooking. It is braised in a rich stock and served as a soup, or even stir-fried. Chinese restaurants sometimes offer a long list of shark's fin dishes. Perhaps more than anything else, it is a blatant symbol of extravagance.

Shark's fin is available dried and sold whole, in pieces or in cleaned strands, in many dry-food shops in China. The fin refers to the dorsal "comb fin" or the two ventral fins of any of a variety of sharks. Indeed, in China, fins are imported from all over the world. Preparation usually involves an elaborate process of soaking and boiling in several changes of water and stocks.

However, thanks to modern technology, one can now purchase prepared shark's fin in the freezer section of Chinese markets. This convenience brings shark's fin within the scope of today's adventurous home cook.

Like bird's nest (see page 53), the other extravagant Chinese delicacy, it has little flavor of its own. However, cooked in a rich, flavorful stock, it is prized for its absorbency, its clear, gelatinous strands, and its texture, which make for an enjoyable combination. It is often served with a rich stock, as in shark's fin soup, or stuffed in poultry, or scrambled with eggs and crab. It also holds high status as a general medicinal tonic.

Price is based on quality. High-quality shark's fin can sometimes be found already prepared and frozen. This is a good buy because all the preparation work has been done and the freezing does not affect the quality or texture of the shark's fin. Keep frozen until ready to use.

If you buy dried shark's fin, store it in a cool, dry place.

NOTE:

To soften dried shark's fin, slowly bring a large pot of cold water with scallions (spring onions) and slices of ginger to a boil. Simmer for at least 2 hours, then allow to cool in the liquid. Rinse carefully, cover in cold water, and refrigerate. The next day, repeat the process. When the shark's fin is soft, it is ready to be paired with a rich stock.

SHRIMP SAUCE OR PASTE

This sauce is made from pulverized, salted shrimp (prawns) that are allowed to ferment. It is available also as shrimp paste, the mixture having been dried in the sun and cut into cakes. As a sauce it is packed in jars in a thick, moist state. Once packed, the light pink shrimp sauce slowly turns a grayish shade, acquiring a pungent flavor as it matures. Popular in southern Chinese cooking, this ingredient adds a distinctive flavor and fragrance to dishes that take some getting used to. The paste is similar to anchovy paste in texture,

though stronger in taste and odor. The cooking process quickly tones down its aroma and taste.

It is available in Chinese supermarkets and grocers. The best brands are from Hong Kong or China (Pearl River Bridge brand).

Kept in the refrigerator, it will last indefinitely.

NOTE:

Don't confuse this sauce with the shrimp paste from Thailand or Malaysia, where a different and milder version is used.

SICHUAN PEPPERCORNS
(ZANTHOXYLUM SIMULANS)

Also known as **fagara, wild pepper, Chinese pepper,** and **anise pepper,** Sichuan peppercorns are an ancient spice known throughout China as "flower peppers" because they look like flower buds that are opening. Used originally and extensively in Sichuan cooking (hence their popular name), they are enjoyed in other parts of China as well. They are a reddish-brown, rusty color with a pungent odor that distinguishes them from the hotter black peppercorns with which they may be used interchangeably. They are the dried berries of a shrub that is a member of the prickly ash tree known as *fagara*. Their smell reminds me of lavender, while their taste is sharp and slightly numbing to the tongue, with a clean, lemon-like, woody spiciness and fragrance.

It is not peppercorns that make Sichuan cooking so hot; rather, it is the chile pepper that creates that sensation. These peppercorns are one of the components of five-spice powder. They can be ground in a conventional pepper mill but should be roasted (see below) before they are ground to bring out their full flavor. Combine them with other peppercorns for additional flavors. They can be used as a part of a dry marinade with salt for grilled meats.

An inexpensive item, they are sold wrapped in cellophane or plastic bags in Chinese stores. Avoid packets with dark seeds; they should be a vibrant reddish-brown color. They are best when the package is vacuum-packed, as the peppers quickly lose their special aroma if left out too long.

They will keep indefinitely in a well-sealed container.

NOTES:

• To roast Sichuan peppercorns, heat a wok or heavy frying pan over medium heat. Add the peppercorns (you can cook up to about 4 ounces or 113 g at a time) and toast them, stirring, for about 3 minutes, or until they brown slightly and start to smoke. Remove the pan from the heat and let them cool.

• Store the peppercorns or grind them in a pepper mill or clean coffee grinder, or with a mortar and pestle. Sift the ground peppercorns through a fine mesh and discard any of the hard hulls. Seal the mixture tightly in a screw-top jar to store.

• To make seasoned salt and pepper, roast Sichuan peppercorns with some sea salt and grind coarsely together. Keep in a glass jar for future use.

SOY SAUCES

Soy sauce was first used in China more than three thousand years ago, when it was a thin, salty liquid in which fragments of fermented soybean floated. Its use has been documented throughout Chinese history, and the process by which it is made has changed many times over the years. One thousand years ago in China, soy sauce was one of the "seven essentials" of daily life, the others being firewood, rice, oil, salt, vinegar, and tea. Today, the type of soy sauce we use has been strained to remove all traces of the bean solids. Soy sauce is an essential ingredient in all types of Asian cooking. It is made from a mixture of soybeans, flour, and water, which is then naturally fermented and aged for some months. The distilled liquid is soy sauce. There are two main types (light and dark), as well as several infused varieties.

The type of soy sauce you use will greatly affect the way a dish will taste. Avoid any soy sauces from Singapore: they are synthetically or chemically manufactured and tend to have a metallic taste. The naturally brewed Japanese soy sauces, especially Kikkoman, are quite popular, have a more complex flavor, and can be substituted for light soy sauce in Chinese cooking.

The best soy sauces to get, however, are the ones imported from either Hong Kong or China. I highly recommend the Koon Chun and Amoy brand from Hong Kong and the Pearl River Bridge brands from China. The soy sauces from Hong Kong tend to be more consistent while the ones from China can often vary in quality. Although the light and dark soy sauce brands from China have similar names, which leads to a lot of confusion, the best way I found to distinguish the two is to shake the bottle. If the sauce is thin, it is the light. If the sauce heavily coats the bottle's sides and is dark in color, you can be sure that it is dark soy sauce. Light and dark soy sauces are often used together in Chinese cooking. They are also wonderful taste additions for sauces and marinades.

Soy sauce will last for quite a long time without refrigeration. However, it is best to keep it tightly sealed and away from light. Because it is already fermented, you don't have to worry about spoilage.

Light Soy Sauce

As the name implies, this is light in color, but it is full of flavor and is the best one to use for cooking. It is known in Chinese markets as Superior Soy and is saltier than dark soy sauce.

Dark Soy Sauce

This sauce is aged for much longer than light soy sauce, hence its darker, almost black color. It is slightly thicker and stronger than light soy sauce and is more suitable for stews. I prefer it to light soy sauce as a dipping sauce. It is known in Chinese markets as Soy Superior Sauce, and although it is used less than light soy sauce, it is important to have some at hand.

Mushroom Soy Sauce

This is a delicious type of black soy sauce that is infused with dried straw mushrooms. The recommended brand is Pearl River Bridge, which is produced in mainland China.

Shrimp-flavored
Soy Sauce

This is primarily an eastern Chinese favorite that is infused with briny dried shrimp (prawns) for an interesting accent.

STAR ANISE

(Illicium verum)

Star anise is the hard, star-shaped seed pod of a small tree that grows in southwestern China. (It is also known as **Chinese anise** or **whole anise**.) It is similar in flavor and fragrance to common anise seed but is more robust and licorice-like. Star anise is an essential ingredient of five-spice powder and, like cinnamon bark, is widely used in braised dishes, to which it imparts a rich taste and fragrance. Star anise has been popular in Europe since the early 1600s.

Buy star anise whole and not broken in pieces. It is sold in plastic packs at Chinese markets and groceries, and is quite inexpensive.

If stored in a tightly covered jar in a cool, dry, dark place, it should keep for many months.

SUGAR

Sugar has been used—sparingly—in the cooking of savory dishes in China for a thousand years. Excessive sugar destroys the palate, but when it is properly employed, sugar helps balance the various flavors of sauces and other dishes. Sugar will keep indefinitely when stored in a dry, cool place. There are many different types of sugar used.

Rock or Yellow Lump Sugar

I particularly like to use rock sugar, which I find to have a richer, more subtle flavor than refined, granulated sugar. It also gives a good luster or glaze to braised "red-cooked" Chinese dishes. It imparts translucence to glazes and sauces. Rock sugar reduced with water makes a good syrup. You may need to break the lumps into smaller pieces with a wooden mallet or rolling pin.

Brown Sugar Slabs

This type of sugar is layered and semirefined, having been compressed into flat slabs and cut to resemble caramel candy. It has the flavor of brown sugar.

Maltose or Malt Sugar

Buy it in Chinese markets, where it is usually sold very inexpensively in packages. If you cannot find it, you may use white sugar or coffee sugar crystals (the amber, chunky kind) instead.

WHEAT GLUTEN

This is made from washing out the starch from wheat dough until only an adhesive, glutinous substance remains. It is usually boiled or deep-fried and then cooked with other ingredients, such as vegetables or sauces. These spongy cakes of gluten dough are often used in Chinese cuisine, but especially in vegetarian cooking, where they form the basis of many "mock meat" dishes. Gluten itself has very little taste, but its virtue is that it readily absorbs the flavors and seasonings of the other ingredients it's cooked with. It is low in fat and high in value.

Wheat gluten can be found in the refrigerated area of Chinese grocers or supermarkets. Canned varieties are available. All brands are rather good, but I would look for brands from Taiwan and China.

If purchased fresh, it should be used within a week. Keep in cold water, changing the water every day.

WONTON WRAPPERS

In China, wonton wrappers and other such doughs were traditionally made painstakingly by hand, the entire extended family engaging in the process while sitting around the main table of the house. Today, there is no need to summon one's entire family from the four corners of the earth. There are very good commercially made wonton wrappers available that can be bought fresh or frozen not only at Chinese markets but increasingly at ordinary supermarkets. They range from very thin to medium pastry-like wrappings that are stretched like freshly made noodles. They can be stuffed with minced meat and then fried, steamed, or used in soups. They are sold in little piles of 3-inch (7.5-cm)—or larger—squares that are wrapped in plastic. The number of squares or skins in a package varies, depending upon the supplier. Buy the very thin ones, if possible.

Wonton wrappers freeze very well; however, they should be well wrapped before freezing. Fresh wrappers will keep for about 5 days if stored in plastic wrap or a plastic bag in the refrigerator. If you are using frozen wonton wrappers, just peel off the number you require and thaw them thoroughly before use. Leave the remainder in the freezer.

NOTES:

• Use your imagination for the filling, which, of course, does not have to be strictly Chinese.

• Try deep-frying them without filling for a wonderful snack with drinks.

RECIPES

SAVORY AMARANTH PORK SOUP

This is a soup my mother made often for our family because it was simple to assemble and a delicious accompaniment to any meal. The pork adds a rich and meaty quality to the broth, which gets its deep red color from the amaranth leaves.

SERVES 4

4 cups (32 fl oz/992 ml) Chicken Stock (page 140) or canned broth

½ pound (227 g) boneless lean pork chops, shredded

1 tablespoon (15 ml) plus 2 teaspoons (10 ml) light soy sauce

4 teaspoons (20 ml) Shaoxing rice wine or dry sherry

½ teaspoon (2.5 ml) dark sesame oil

½ teaspoon (2.5 ml) cornstarch (cornflour)

1 tablespoon (15 ml) peanut (groundnut) oil

1 pound (454 g) fresh amaranth leaves, washed and drained

1 teaspoon (5 ml) dark soy sauce

Salt and freshly ground pepper

2 scallions (spring onions), finely chopped

Bring the stock to a boil in a medium-sized pot and let simmer.

In a medium-sized bowl, combine the pork with 1 tablespoon (15 ml) of the light soy sauce, 2 teaspoons (10 ml) of the rice wine, the sesame oil, and the cornstarch. Heat a wok or large frying pan over high heat until it is hot, and add the peanut oil. When the oil is slightly smoking, add the pork mixture and stir-fry for 1 minute. Remove from the heat and set aside.

Add the amaranth, the remaining 2 teaspoons (10 ml) of rice wine, the dark soy sauce, and the remaining 2 teaspoons (10 ml) of light soy sauce to the simmering stock. Let simmer for 5 minutes. Return the pork to the stock and simmer for another minute. Season with salt and pepper to taste. Transfer to a large soup tureen or individual soup bowls. Garnish with the scallions and serve at once.

STIR-FRIED SILK SQUASH WITH GINGER AND OYSTER SAUCE

This easy-to-prepare dish makes a savory vegetable accompaniment for any menu. The silk squash, which tastes like a cross between zucchini (courgette) and cucumber, absorbs the sauce like a sponge.

SERVES 4

1½ pounds (680 g) silk squash

2 tablespoons (30 ml) peanut (groundnut) oil

2 tablespoons (30 ml) finely shredded fresh ginger

2 cloves garlic, finely sliced

3 tablespoons (44 ml) oyster sauce

½ cup (4 fl oz/118 ml) Chicken Stock (page 140) or canned broth

Peel away the tough outer skin of the squash and cut the meat in half lengthwise and then into 2-inch (5-cm) pieces. Heat a wok or large frying pan over high heat until it is hot, and add the oil. When the oil is slightly smoking, add in the ginger, garlic, and squash. Stir-fry for 2 minutes, then add the oyster sauce and stock. Simmer uncovered until the squash is tender, about 5 minutes. Serve at once.

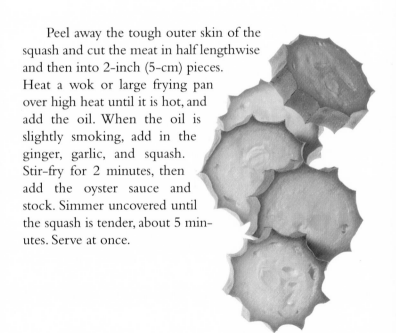

CHINESE EGGPLANT WITH CHICKEN IN HOISIN AND CHILE BEAN SAUCE

Here's a hearty dish that can easily be the main course of any meal. It is flavorful and aromatic, and much of the preparation work can be done ahead of time. This dish also reheats well.

SERVES 4

2 pounds (907 g) Chinese or other eggplant (aubergine)

½ pound (227 g) skinless, boneless chicken thigh or breast, coarsely chopped

1 tablespoon (15 ml) plus 1 teaspoon (5 ml) light soy sauce

1 tablespoon (15 ml) Shaoxing rice wine

1¼ teaspoons (6 ml) sugar

1 teaspoon (5 ml) dark sesame oil

¼ teaspoon (1 ml) salt

¼ teaspoon (1 ml) freshly ground pepper

1 teaspoon (5 ml) cornstarch (cornflour)

½ tablespoon (7 ml) peanut (groundnut) oil

2 scallions (spring onions), finely chopped

3 cloves garlic, finely sliced

1 tablespoon (15 ml) finely chopped fresh ginger

2 teaspoons (10 ml) finely chopped orange zest

2 teaspoons (10 ml) chile bean sauce

1 tablespoon (15 ml) hoisin sauce

2 teaspoons (10 ml) dark soy sauce

Preheat the oven to 475°F (245°C).

Roast the eggplant whole for 20 minutes (if you are using large eggplant, roast them for 30 to 40 minutes), or until they are soft and cooked through. Allow them to cool and then peel them. Put them in a colander and let them drain for at least 30 minutes. Pull them apart into strands. (This procedure can be done hours in advance.)

In a bowl, combine the chicken with 1 teaspoon (5 ml) of the light soy sauce, 1 teaspoon (5 ml) of the rice wine, ¼ teaspoon (1 ml) of the sugar, and the sesame oil, salt, pepper, and cornstarch.

Heat a wok or large frying pan over high heat until it is hot. Add the peanut oil, then the scallions, garlic, ginger, and orange zest, and stir-fry for 2 minutes. Add the chicken mixture and stir-fry for another 2 minutes. Add the eggplant, bean sauce, hoisin sauce, the remaining 1 tablespoon (15 ml) of light soy sauce, the remaining 2 teaspoons (10 ml) of rice wine, the remaining 1 teaspoon (5 ml) of sugar, and the dark soy sauce, and cook for another 3 minutes, stirring occasionally. Give the mixture one last good stir, pour onto a platter, and serve at once.

WOK-FRIED FISH WITH BLACK BEAN SAUCE

In Hong Kong, this Cantonese-style technique is a popular way to prepare fish. The rich flavors of the black beans enhance all types of seafood—especially fish—so don't hesitate to experiment. The sauce can be assembled ahead of time and quickly reheated.

Serves 4

1 teaspoon (5 ml) salt

¼ teaspoon (1 ml) freshly ground pepper

4 fillets (about 4 ounces/113 g each) of sole (bream) or other flat fish

Cornstarch (cornflour) for dusting

2 to 3 tablespoons (30 to 44 ml) peanut (groundnut) oil

THE BLACK BEAN SAUCE

1 tablespoon (15 ml) peanut (groundnut) oil

2 tablespoons (30 ml) coarsely chopped black beans

1 tablespoon (15 ml) finely chopped ginger

2 cloves garlic, finely chopped

1 shallot, finely chopped

3 scallions (spring onions), finely chopped

1½ tablespoons (22 ml) Shaoxing rice wine
    or dry sherry

⅓ cup (2.6 fl oz/78 ml) Chicken Stock (page 140)
    or water

2 teaspoons (10 ml) light soy sauce

1 tablespoon (15 ml) dark soy sauce

Pinch salt

Pinch freshly ground pepper

2 tablespoons (30 ml) cornstarch (cornflour) mixed
    with 1 tablespoon (15 ml) cold water

2 teaspoons (10 ml) dark sesame oil

Sprinkle the salt and pepper evenly over the fish fillets and dust them with cornstarch, shaking off any excess. Turn the oven to a low setting and place a serving platter in it to warm.

Heat a wok or large frying pan over high heat until it is hot, and add 1½ tablespoons (22 ml) of oil. When the oil is slightly smoking, turn the heat to low, add the fillets, and pan-fry for 2 minutes, or until they are crispy and brown. Add more of the oil, if necessary. Turn them over and brown the other side. Transfer the fish to paper towels to drain. Turn off the oven and place the fish in the oven on the platter.

To make the sauce, wipe the wok clean and reheat it. When it is hot, add the oil, black beans, ginger, garlic, shallot, and half of the scallions and stir-fry for 2 minutes. Then add the rice wine, stock, soy sauces, salt, and pepper. Bring the mixture to the boil. Lower the heat, add the cornstarch mixture, and simmer for 1 minute. Add the sesame oil and mix well. Pour the sauce over the fish. Garnish with the remaining scallions. Serve at once.

CHICKEN WITH BROCCOLI AND CITRUS PEEL

This hearty and healthful combination is accented by the pungent taste of dried citrus peel. Chicken thighs are best for this recipe because they can withstand the long cooking time required for the meat to absorb the sauce.

SERVES 4

THE CHICKEN AND BROCCOLI

1 pound (454 g) boneless, skinless chicken thighs, cut into 2-inch (5-cm) pieces

1 tablespoon (15 ml) light soy sauce

2 teaspoons (10 ml) Shaoxing rice wine or dry sherry

1 teaspoon (5 ml) salt

½ teaspoon (2.5 ml) freshly ground pepper

1 teaspoon (5 ml) dark sesame oil

2 teaspoons (10 ml) cornstarch (cornflour)

1 pound (454 g) fresh broccoli

THE SAUCE

1½ tablespoons (22 ml) peanut (groundnut) oil

3 cloves garlic, finely sliced

2 tablespoons (30 ml) finely shredded ginger

2 tablespoons (30 ml) dried citrus peel, soaked and finely chopped

1 teaspoon (5 ml) salt

½ teaspoon (2.5 ml) freshly ground pepper

2 to 3 tablespoons (30 to 44 ml) water

1 tablespoon (15 ml) chile bean sauce

2 teaspoons (10 ml) dark sesame oil

In a medium-sized bowl, combine the chicken pieces with the soy sauce, rice wine, salt, pepper, sesame oil, and cornstarch. Mix well and let marinate for at least 30 minutes in the refrigerator.

Bring a large pot of salted water to a boil. Separate the broccoli heads into small florets, and peel and slice the stems. Add the broccoli florets and stems to the pot and blanch for several minutes. Drain, then shock them in cold water to prevent further cooking. Drain thoroughly and set aside.

To prepare the sauce, heat a wok or large frying pan over high heat until it is hot, then add the oil. When the oil is slightly smoking, add the garlic, ginger, citrus peel, salt, and pepper. Stir-fry for a few seconds, add the chicken, and stir-fry for 4 minutes, or until the chicken is browned. Add the broccoli and the water. Stir-fry at a moderate to high heat for 4 minutes, until the chicken is cooked and the broccoli is thoroughly heated through. Add the chile bean sauce and sesame oil and continue to stir-fry for 2 minutes. Serve at once.

DOUBLE-BOILED BIRD'S NEST SOUP

This soup is a classic banquet dish served with great fanfare. Since birds' nests are expensive, the soup is always savored slowly and highly prized for its gelatinous texture. There's no way to reduce the long preparation time without compromising results, but the good news is that the soup reheats well.

Serves 4

1 cup (237 ml) dried bird's nest, soaked 8 to 10 hours or overnight

1 chicken (3 to 3½ pounds/1.4 to 1.6 kg), cut into quarters

6 cups (48 fl oz/1.4 l) Chicken Stock (page 140) or canned broth

4 whole scallions (spring onions)

4 thick slices ginger (1 by 1½ inches/2.5 by 4 cm)

2 tablespoons (30 ml) Shaoxing rice wine or dry sherry

Salt

Freshly ground white pepper

2 egg whites

2 teaspoons (10 ml) dark sesame oil

Bring a large pot of water to a boil. Add the bird's nest and the chicken and boil for 10 minutes. Drain and rinse under cold running water. Drain again, and set aside.

Bring the chicken stock to a boil in a large pot. Add the chicken, scallions, ginger, bird's nest, and rice wine. Pour the mixture into a 2-quart (1.9-l) heatproof casserole. Cover the casserole and set it inside a large steamer. Steam over gently simmering water on a rack in a tightly covered wok or pot for 1 hour, replenishing the hot water as necessary.

Remove the chicken and any surface fat, reserving the chicken for another use. Adjust the seasoning of the stock to taste with salt and white pepper. In a small bowl, mix the egg whites with the sesame oil and slowly pour the mixture into the stock, stirring slowly. Pour into a soup tureen and serve at once.

STIR-FRIED SHARK'S FIN WITH EGGS

Shark's fin has a crunchy texture that is enhanced and high-lighted in this unusual recipe. The bacon gives the dish a smoky, salty taste and the eggs help unite all the elements.

SERVES 2 TO 4

6 eggs, beaten

2 teaspoons (10 ml) dark sesame oil

1 teaspoon (5 ml) salt

1½ tablespoons (22 ml) peanut (groundnut) oil

4 ounces (113 g) bacon, finely shredded

½ pound (227 g) prepared shark's fin, thawed

6 scallions (spring onions), sliced

In a medium-sized bowl, mix the eggs with the sesame oil and salt and set aside.

Heat a wok or large frying pan over high heat until it is hot, and swirl in the peanut oil. When the oil is slightly smoking, toss in the bacon and shark's fin and stir-fry for 3 minutes. Add the egg mixture and stir-fry until the egg begins to set, about 5 minutes. Toss in the scallions and stir-fry another minute. Quickly transfer to a platter and serve at once.

NOTE:

If you are using dried shark's fin, soak it 8 to 10 hours or overnight, then simmer it with 4 slices of ginger and 4 whole scallions for 2 hours, or until soft, before proceeding with the recipe.

STIR-FRIED WATER SPINACH WITH GARLIC

Quick stir-frying is the best way to bring out the earthy flavors of water spinach. The garlic is used to flavor the oil before the spinach goes into the hot wok. This makes a good vegetable side dish.

SERVES 4

1½ pounds (680 g) fresh water spinach

1 tablespoon (15 ml) peanut (groundnut) oil

3 cloves garlic, finely sliced

1 teaspoon (5 ml) salt

1 teaspoon (5 ml) sugar

Wash the water spinach thoroughly. Remove all the tough stems, leaving just the tender stems and leaves.

Heat a wok or large frying pan over high heat until it is hot and add the oil. When the oil is slightly smoking, add the garlic and salt. Stir-fry for 10 seconds, then add the water spinach. Stir-fry for about 2 minutes to thoroughly coat the water spinach. When the water spinach is wilted to about one third of its original volume, add the sugar and stir-fry for 4 more minutes. Transfer the water spinach to a plate and pour off any excess liquid. Serve at once.

STIR-FRIED BITTER MELON WITH BEEF

Bitter melon is an acquired taste, even among Asians. However, I find its slightly bitter flavors somewhat addicting and use it to balance dishes that feature rich meats, such as beef. Serve this as a main course with rice and a vegetable dish.

SERVES 4

- 1 pound (454 g) bitter melon
- 1 tablespoon (15 ml) peanut (groundnut) oil
- 3 cloves garlic, coarsely chopped
- ½ pound (227 g) ground beef
- 2 tablespoons (30 ml) light soy sauce
- 1 tablespoon (15 ml) Shaoxing rice wine or dry sherry
- 2 teaspoons (10 ml) sugar
- 1 teaspoon (5 ml) salt
- 3 tablespoons (44 ml) Chicken Stock (page 140) or water
- 2 teaspoons (10 ml) dark sesame oil

Slice the bitter melon in half lengthwise. Remove the seeds and finely chop the melon. Blanch the bitter melon in boiling water for 2 minutes and drain thoroughly.

Heat a wok or large frying pan over high heat until it is hot. Add the oil and the garlic, and stir-fry for 30 seconds. Add the beef and stir-fry for 2 minutes. Add the soy sauce, rice wine, sugar, salt, bitter melon, and stock, and stir-fry for another 4 minutes, or until the beef is cooked. Stir in the sesame oil, turn onto a serving platter, and serve.

STIR-FRIED RICE NOODLES WITH YELLOW CHIVES

Dried rice noodles are a perfect convenience food for most Asians. Simply soak them in warm water until soft, drain, then stir-fry. Here I have combined them with yellow chives, which have a subtle garlic-like bite.

SERVES 4

THE NOODLES AND CHIVES

½ pound (227 g) dried rice noodles

¼ pound (113 g) ground pork

2 teaspoons (10 ml) Shaoxing rice wine
    or dry sherry

1 teaspoon (5 ml) light soy sauce

½ teaspoon (2.5 ml) dark sesame oil

½ teaspoon (2.5 ml) cornstarch (cornflour)

2½ tablespoons (37 ml) peanut (groundnut) oil

2 cloves garlic, coarsely chopped

1 pound (454 g) Chinese yellow chives, cut into
    3-inch (8-cm) pieces

THE SAUCE

3 tablespoons (44 ml) oyster sauce

1½ tablespoons (22 ml) Shaoxing rice wine
    or dry sherry

1 tablespoon (15 ml) light soy sauce

1 tablespoon (15 ml) dark soy sauce

3 tablespoons (44 ml) Chicken Stock (page 140)
    or water

1 teaspoon (5 ml) salt

¼ teaspoon (1 ml) freshly ground pepper

1 teaspoon (5 ml) sugar

1 tablespoon (15 ml) dark sesame oil

Soak the dried rice noodles in warm water for 20 minutes. Drain thoroughly and set aside.

In a small bowl, combine the pork with the rice wine, soy sauce, ½ teaspoon (2.5 ml) of sesame oil, and corn-starch.

Heat a wok or large frying pan over high heat until it is hot. Add 1 tablespoon (15 ml) of the peanut oil and the garlic. When the garlic has slightly browned, about 15 seconds, add the pork mixture and stir-fry for 2 minutes. Remove the pork and garlic with a slotted spoon and set aside.

Reheat the wok and add the remaining 1½ tablespoons (22 ml) of peanut oil. When it is very hot, add the rice noodles and chives, and stir-fry for 30 seconds.

Add the oyster sauce, rice wine, soy sauces, chicken stock, salt, pepper, and sugar to the wok. Stir-fry over medium heat for 5 minutes. Return the pork to the wok and mix well, stir-frying for another minute. Give the mixture several good stirs and add the sesame oil. Turn onto a platter and serve.

SESAME NOODLES

This popular Sichuan-Beijing dish can be served as a quick snack. The sesame paste gives the noodles a rich peanut coating. Served cold, it makes a delightful summer dish.

SERVES 4

½ pound (227 g) fresh or dried Chinese egg noodles

1 tablespoon (15 ml) dark sesame oil

1 fresh red chile, seeded and coarsely chopped

2 teaspoons (10 ml) peanut (groundnut) oil

2 tablespoons (30 ml) sesame paste

2 tablespoons (30 ml) orange juice

1 scallion (spring onion), finely chopped

2 cloves garlic, chopped

1 tablespoon (15 ml) Chinese white rice vinegar
or cider vinegar

1 tablespoon (15 ml) light soy sauce

1 teaspoon salt

Pinch freshly ground pepper

2 teaspoons (10 ml) sugar

2 teaspoons (10 ml) Chile Oil (page 139)

Bring a large pot of water to a boil. Add the noodles and cook for 3 to 5 minutes. Drain well and plunge them immediately in cold water. Drain again and immediately toss them with the sesame oil.

Combine the remaining ingredients together in a bowl or an electric blender. (This sauce can be prepared in advance and kept refrigerated, as it is to be served cold.) Toss the noodles well with the sauce just before serving.

SIMPLE STIR-FRIED CHINESE LONGBEANS

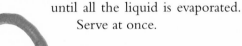

In this dish, delectable and crunchy Chinese longbeans are simply stir-fried over high heat to seal in their natural flavors. They are merely enhanced by salt, pepper, and a touch of water, which keeps them moist.

SERVES 2 TO 4

- 1½ tablespoons (22 ml) peanut (groundnut) oil
- 1 pound (454 g) Chinese longbeans, trimmed and sliced diagonally into bite-sized pieces
- 2 teaspoons (10 ml) salt
- ½ teaspoon (2.5 ml) freshly ground pepper
- 1 teaspoon (5 ml) sugar
- 3 tablespoons (44 ml) water

Heat a wok or large frying-pan over high heat until it is hot, and add the oil. When the oil is slightly smoking, add the beans and stir-fry for 30 seconds. Add the salt, pepper, sugar, and water and continue to stir-fry for 1 minute. Cover the wok and cook the beans for 5 minutes, or until soft. Uncover, and continue to stir-fry until all the liquid is evaporated. Serve at once.

BRAISED CHICKEN WITH TREE EARS

Here I have combined chicken with crunchy tree ears. It is a traditional dish served in many Chinese homes, possibly because braised dishes like this one reheat easily and are ideal components of multicourse family meals.

SERVES 4

I pound (454 g) boneless, skinless chicken thighs,
   cut into bite-sized pieces

5 teaspoons (25 ml) light soy sauce

5 teaspoons (25 ml) Shaoxing rice wine or dry sherry

I teaspoon (5 ml) dark sesame oil

½ teaspoon (2.5 ml) salt

¼ teaspoon (I ml) freshly ground pepper

I teaspoon (5 ml) cornstarch (cornflour)

¼ cup (59 ml or 2 ounces/57 g) tree ears

2 tablespoons (30 ml) peanut (groundnut) oil

4 cloves garlic, coarsely chopped

I tablespoon (I5 ml) dark soy sauce

2 teaspoons (I0 ml) sugar

I cup (8 fl oz/237 ml) Chicken Stock (page I40)
   or canned broth

I teaspoon (5 ml) cornstarch (cornflour) mixed with
   2 teaspoons (I0 ml) water

In a medium-sized bowl, combine the chicken with 3 teaspoons (15 ml) of the light soy sauce, 2 teaspoons (10 ml) of the rice wine, the sesame oil, salt, pepper, and cornstarch. Let it sit for 20 minutes.

Soak the tree ears in warm water for 20 minutes, or until they are soft. Rinse under running water to remove any remaining sand. With a sharp knife, remove the hard stems and discard. Shred the tree ears and set aside.

Heat a wok or large frying pan over high heat until it is hot. Add the oil and garlic, and stir-fry for 1 minute. Add the chicken, and stir-fry for 2 minutes. Pour the contents into a clay pot or casserole, along with the tree ears, the remaining 2 teaspoons (10 ml) of light soy sauce, the remaining 3 teaspoons (15 ml) of rice wine, and the dark soy sauce, sugar, and chicken stock. Bring the mixture to a boil. Lower the heat, cover, and simmer for 15 minutes. Remove the cover, and pour in the cornstarch mixture. Cook uncovered, stirring, until the sauce thickens, about 2 minutes. Serve at once.

RED PORK WITH CHINESE WHITE RADISH

This full-flavored, satisfying family-style dish gets its robust taste—spices permeate the meat and radish—through slow cooking. This dish reheats well and makes a delightful cold-weather meal.

SERVES 4 TO 6

- 1 pork shoulder (3 to 4 pounds/1.4 to 1.8 kg), bones in with rind
- 3 whole star anise
- 2 pieces cinnamon bark, or 2 cinnamon sticks
- 3 dried red chiles
- 2 cups (473 ml) Shaoxing rice wine or dry sherry
- 3 cups (710 ml) Chicken Stock (page 140) or canned broth
- 1 cup (237 ml) dark soy sauce
- ½ cup (118 ml) light soy sauce
- ½ cup (118 ml) rock sugar, or ¼ cup (59 ml) granulated sugar
- 5 thin slices ginger
- 8 cloves garlic, peeled and crushed
- 6 whole scallions (spring onions)
- 2 teaspoons (10 ml) salt
- 1 teaspoon (5 ml) freshly ground pepper
- 2 pounds (907 g) Chinese white radish, peeled and slant cut into 2-inch (5-cm) pieces

Bring a large pot of water to the boil and add the pork shoulder. When it comes to a boil again, skim the fat, and reduce the heat. Simmer gently, partially covered, for 30 minutes. Drain thoroughly.

Place the star anise, cinnamon, and dried chiles in a cheesecloth and tie tightly to close. Combine the rice wine, chicken stock, soy sauces, sugar, ginger, garlic, scallions, salt, and pepper in a very large pot and bring the liquid to a simmer. Add the spices in the cheesecloth and the pork shoulder, and return the liquid to a simmer, partially covered, skimming constantly. Cover the pot tightly and continue to simmer gently for 2 hours, until the pork fat and rind are very soft and tender.

Add the radish to the pot and continue to simmer for another hour, or until both the pork and radish are tender. Skim all the fat. Reduce the liquid to a syrup and serve with the pork.

LEMONGRASS CHICKEN

Lemongrass, with its subtle citrus aroma, is the perfect partner for chicken. Inspired by a Vietnamese cook, I have combined it with ginger and chiles for a mouthwatering main course.

SERVES 4

5 stalks fresh lemongrass

1 pound (454 g) boneless, skinless chicken thighs, blotted dry and cut into 1-inch (2.5-cm) pieces

1 teaspoon (5 ml) salt

½ teaspoon (2.5 ml) freshly ground pepper

3 cloves garlic, coarsely chopped

3 scallions (spring onions), finely chopped

1 tablespoon (15 ml) peanut (groundnut) oil

1 large red (Spanish) onion, finely sliced

1 tablespoon (15 ml) finely chopped ginger

2 small red or green chiles, seeded and coarsely chopped

2 teaspoons (10 ml) sugar

Peel the lemongrass down to the tender whitish center of the stalk, crush the stalk, and cut it into 3-inch (8-cm) pieces. In a large bowl, combine the chicken with the lemongrass, salt, pepper, garlic, and scallions, and allow to marinate at room temperature for 1 hour.

Heat a wok or large frying pan over high heat until it is hot and add the oil. When the oil is slightly smoking, turn the heat to low. Add the chicken and marinade to the wok and stir-fry for 5 minutes.

Add the onion, ginger, and chiles, and stir-fry for 10 minutes. Add the sugar and continue to stir-fry for 5 minutes. Transfer to a platter and serve at once.

HOISIN-MARINATED SPARERIBS

With its rich sweetness, hoisin marries well with other seasonings, such as barbecue sauces. Used with pork spareribs, it makes a truly delicious match. The first cooking removes fat and tenderizes the spareribs.

SERVES 4

3½ pounds (1.6 kg) pork spareribs

THE MARINADE

1½ cloves garlic, finely chopped

1 tablespoon (15 ml) finely chopped ginger

2 tablespoons (30 ml) light soy sauce

2 tablespoons (30 ml) dark soy sauce

3 tablespoons (44 ml) Shaoxing rice wine
   or dry sherry

3 tablespoons (44 ml) chile bean sauce

1 tablespoon (15 ml) dark sesame oil

2 teaspoons (10 ml) salt

1 teaspoon (5 ml) freshly ground pepper

2 tablespoons (30 ml) sugar

5 tablespoons (74 ml) hoisin sauce

Mix the marinade ingredients together and lay the spareribs on a baking sheet. Spread the marinade evenly on both sides of the spareribs. Wrap with plastic wrap and refrigerate 8 to 10 hours.

Preheat the oven to 250°F (120°C).

Place the ribs in the oven and cook for 2 hours and 15 minutes. Pour off any excess fat.

Turn the temperature to 450°F (230°C) and cook for another 10 minutes. Serve at once.

SICHUAN PEPPERCORN BEEF

Peppercorns have one of the most recognizable smells of Sichuan cuisine, probably because they are tossed into almost every dish. And no wonder—they always add a fragrance and bold flavor that's unbeatable. They also stand up to beef very well.

SERVES 4

- 1 pound (454 g) New York (rump) steak
- 1 tablespoon (15 ml) light soy sauce
- 4 teaspoons (20 ml) dark sesame oil
- 2 tablespoons (30 ml) Shaoxing rice wine or dry sherry
- 2 teaspoons (10 ml) cornstarch (cornflour)
- ¼ cup (59 ml) peanut (groundnut) oil
- 3 cloves garlic, coarsely chopped
- 3 scallions (spring onions), finely chopped
- 2 teaspoons (10 ml) chile bean sauce
- 1 teaspoon (5 ml) salt
- ½ teaspoon (2.5 ml) freshly ground pepper
- 1 teaspoon (5 ml) sugar
- 2 teaspoons (10 ml) roasted and ground Sichuan peppercorns (page 96)

Cut the beef into 2 by ¼-inch (5 by 1-cm) slices and put them into a bowl. Add the soy sauce, 2 teaspoons (10 ml) of the sesame oil, 1 tablespoon (15 ml) of the rice wine, and the cornstarch. Let the mixture marinate for 20 minutes.

Heat a wok or large frying pan over high heat until it is hot, and add 3 tablespoons (44 ml) of the peanut oil. When the oil is slightly smoking, add the beef slices and stir-fry for 5 minutes, or until they are lightly browned. Drain them well in a colander resting in a bowl. Discard the oil.

Wipe the wok or pan clean and reheat it over high heat until it is hot. Add the remaining 1 tablespoon (15 ml) of peanut oil, then add the garlic and scallions, and stir-fry for 30 seconds. Add the remaining 1 tablespoon (15 ml) of rice wine and the bean sauce and stir-fry for another 15 seconds. Add the drained beef, salt, pepper, sugar, remaining 2 teaspoons (10 ml) of sesame oil, and the peppercorns, and toss thoroughly. Turn the mixture onto a serving platter and serve at once.

SPICY SHRIMP-FLAVORED CHICKEN

Here's an unusual match that works remarkably well. Once shrimp paste is cooked and combined with other ingredients, its sharpness mellows and creates a tasty sauce.

SERVES 4

1 pound (454 g) boneless, skinless chicken thighs, cut into 1-inch (2.5 cm) pieces

1 teaspoon (5 ml) salt

2 tablespoons (30 ml) plus 1 teaspoon (5 ml) peanut (groundnut) oil

3 dried red chiles, halved lengthwise

4 scallions (spring onions), cut into 2-inch (5-cm) pieces

2 teaspoons (10 ml) finely chopped fresh ginger

1 tablespoon (15 ml) chile bean sauce

1 tablespoon (15 ml) shrimp paste

½ cup (4 fl oz/118 g) Chicken Stock (page 140) or canned broth

2 teaspoons (10 ml) sugar

½ teaspoon (2.5 ml) freshly ground pepper

Rub the chicken thighs with the salt and let them sit for about 30 minutes.

Heat a wok or large frying pan over high heat until it is hot and add 2 tablespoons of the oil. When the oil is slightly smoking, add the dried chiles and stir to flavor the oil. When the oil turns black, turn down the heat. Add the chicken pieces and slowly brown. Drain the cooked pieces in a colander resting in a stainless bowl, then transfer to paper towels.

Clean the wok over medium heat and reheat it. When it is hot, add the remaining 1 teaspoon (5 ml) of oil. Add the scallions, ginger, bean sauce, and shrimp paste, regulating the heat so the sauce will not burn. A few seconds later, add the chicken stock, sugar, and pepper. Turn the heat down low, return the chicken to the wok, and cover. Cook the chicken in the sauce until done, about 15 minutes, turning the pieces from time to time. Skim off any surface fat and serve the chicken with the sauce.

STIR-FRIED CHINESE CELERY WITH FERMENTED BEAN CURD

Fermented bean curd, a pungent condiment, is often used to give vegetables an added punch. In this recipe, I have combined it with Chinese celery, which is very crispy. The result is a hearty and flavorful vegetarian dish.

SERVES 4

1½ pounds (680 g) Chinese celery

1 tablespoon (15 ml) peanut (groundnut) oil

3 cloves garlic, finely sliced

2 tablespoons (30 ml) fermented bean curd

3 tablespoons (44 ml) Shaoxing rice wine or dry sherry

2 teaspoons (10 ml) chile bean sauce

6 tablespoons (89 ml) water

Break apart the celery stalks and rinse them and their leaves thoroughly under cold running water. Chop the stalks and leaves into 1-inch- (2.5-cm-) wide pieces.

Heat a wok or large frying-pan over high heat until it is hot, and add the oil. When it is slightly smoking, add the garlic, bean curd, and celery, and stir-fry for 2 minutes. Add the rice wine, bean sauce, and water, and continue to stir-fry for 5 minutes, or until the celery is cooked. Transfer to a serving dish and serve at once.

SHRIMP ROLLS

These crispy, transparent rolls are a perfect appetizer. Although the rolls can be made in advance, they are best cooked just before serving. The filling melds together and the result is simply delicious. Don't pass over this recipe just because you haven't worked with rice papers. They're easier to handle than you might think.

MAKES 16 ROLLS

- 2 tablespoons (30 ml) salt
- ½ pound (227 g) shrimp (prawns), peeled and deveined
- 1 tablespoon (15 ml) dark sesame oil
- 2 tablespoons (30 ml) finely chopped fresh coriander
- 2 scallions (spring onions), finely chopped
- 4 ounces (113 g) bean thread noodles, soaked, drained, and finely chopped
- Salt and freshly ground pepper
- 1 package rice paper rounds
- 2 cups (473 ml) peanut (groundnut) oil

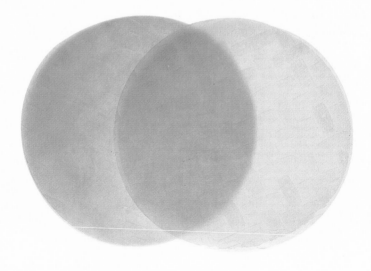

Fill a large bowl with cold water, add 1 tablespoon (15 ml) of the salt, and gently wash the shrimp in the water. Drain and repeat the process. Rinse the shrimp under cold running water, drain, and blot them dry with paper towels.

Combine the shrimp with the sesame oil, coriander, scallions, and bean thread noodles. Mix well, season with salt and pepper to taste, and cover with plastic wrap. Let the mixture sit in the refrigerator for about 1 hour.

When you are ready to make the shrimp rolls, fill a large bowl with warm water. Dip a rice paper in the water and let it soften a few seconds. Transfer to a linen towel to drain.

Place one shrimp with about 1 teaspoon (5 ml) of noodles on the edge of the rice paper. Roll the edge over the shrimp and noodles at once, fold up both ends of the rice paper, and continue to roll to the end. (The roll should be compact and tight, rather like a short, thick cigar, about 3 inches/8 cm long.) Set the roll on a clean plate and continue the process until you have used up all the mixture.

Heat the peanut oil in a wok or deep frying pan until it is moderately hot, about 350°F (175°C), and deep-fry the rolls a few at a time. (They have a tendency to stick to each other at the beginning of the frying, so do only a few at a time.) Drain them on paper towels and serve at once.

NOTE:

The shrimp rolls can be assembled in advance, covered with plastic wrap, and refrigerated for up to 4 hours before deep-frying.

MU SHU-STYLE CHICKEN

Mu shu is a popular western and northern Chinese dish that is usually made with pork, but I have found that chicken works just as well. It is fun to eat, as each diner helps himself or herself to a pancake, sauce, and the chicken mixture.

SERVES 4

1 pound (454 g) boneless, skinless, chicken thighs, cut into thin, 3-inch- (8-cm-) long strips

6½ teaspoons (32 ml) light soy sauce

5 teaspoons (25 ml) Shaoxing rice wine or dry sherry

2 teaspoons (10 ml) salt

1 teaspoon (5 ml) cornstarch (cornflour)

½ ounce (14 g) dried lily stems, soaked

¼ cup (59 ml or 2 ounces/57 g) tree ears, soaked

5½ tablespoons (83 ml) peanut (groundnut) oil

4 eggs, beaten

6 scallions (spring onions), finely shredded

1 teaspoon (5 ml) sugar

1 teaspoon (5 ml) freshly ground pepper

2 teaspoons (10 ml) dark sesame oil

Chinese Pancakes (recipe follows)

Hoisin sauce, for dipping

In a medium-sized bowl, combine the chicken strips with 2 teaspoons (10 ml) of the soy sauce, 2 teaspoons (10 ml) of the rice wine, 1 teaspoon (5 ml) of the salt, and the cornstarch, and refrigerate for about 20 minutes.

Trim the hard ends of the lily stems and shred them by pulling them apart. Rinse the tree ears in several changes of water, remove the hard stems, and finely shred.

Heat a wok or large frying pan over high heat until it is hot, and add 2 tablespoons of the oil. Add the chicken mixture and stir-fry for 5 minutes. Drain the chicken in a colander and discard the oil.

Wipe the wok clean and heat it again until it is hot. Add 2 more tablespoons (30 ml) of the oil. Immediately add the eggs and gently stir-fry them by lifting them up and around until they are set. Transfer the eggs immediately to paper towels to drain.

Wipe the wok clean again and reheat. When it is very hot, add the remaining 1½ tablespoons (22 ml) of oil. Add the lily stems, tree ears, and scallions, and stir-fry for 1 minute. Add the remaining 4½ teaspoons of soy sauce, the sugar, pepper, and sesame oil, and stir-fry for another 2 minutes. Return the cooked chicken and egg to the wok and stir-fry the mixture for another 2 minutes, mixing thoroughly. Place chicken mixture, Chinese pancakes, and hoisin sauce in separate serving dishes and serve at once.

CHINESE PANCAKES

MAKES 18 PANCAKES

2 cups (473 ml) unbleached all-purpose (plain) flour

4 cups (992 ml) very hot water

2 tablespoons (30 ml) dark sesame oil

Put the flour into a large bowl. Using chopsticks, gradually stir the hot water into the flour, mixing continuously until the water is fully incorporated. (Add more water if the mixture seems dry.) Remove the mixture from the bowl and knead it until it is smooth, about 8 minutes. Put the dough back into the bowl, cover it with a clean, damp towel, and let it rest for about 30 minutes.

After the dough has rested, knead it again until smooth, about 5 minutes, dusting it with a little flour if it is sticky. Form it into an 18-inch- (46-cm-) long by 1-inch- (2.5-cm-) in-diameter roll. With a knife, cut the roll into 18 equal segments. Roll each segment into a ball.

Take two of the dough balls. Dip one side of one ball into the sesame oil and place the oiled side on top of the other ball. Using a rolling pin, roll the two balls into one circle about 6 inches (15 cm) in diameter. (It is important to roll double pancakes in this way because the resulting dough will remain moist inside and you will be able to roll them thinner while avoiding the risk of overcooking them.)

Heat a wok or large frying pan over a very low heat. Put the double pancake into the wok and cook it until it has dried on one side. Flip it over and cook the other side. Remove from the pan, peel the two pancakes apart, and set them aside. Repeat this process until all the dough balls have been cooked.

To reheat the pancakes, steam by wrapping them tightly in a double sheet of foil and placing them in a pan containing 1 inch (2.5 cm) of boiling water. Cover the pan, turn down the heat very low, and simmer until the pancakes are reheated. If well wrapped, the pancakes can also be reheated in the microwave. (Don't be tempted to reheat them in the oven, as this will dry them out.)

NOTE:

If you want to freeze the cooked pancakes, wrap them tightly in plastic wrap first. When using pancakes that have been frozen, let them thaw in the refrigerator before reheating them.

STIR-FRIED VEGETARIAN WHEAT GLUTEN

Buddhist restaurants all over Asia serve this dish. Wheat gluten provides the substance in many vegetarian dishes. When it is combined with a variety of sauces, it assumes a rich full-bodied texture that satisfies vegetarians and nonvegetarians alike.

SERVES 4

½ pound (227 g) fresh or canned wheat gluten

1½ tablespoons (22 ml) peanut (groundnut) oil

3 cloves garlic, coarsely chopped

½ teaspoon salt

Pinch freshly ground pepper

¼ cup (59 ml or 2 ounces/57 g) cloud ears, soaked and rinsed

¼ cup (59 ml) water or Chicken Stock (page 140)

2 tablespoons (30 ml) Shaoxing rice wine or dry sherry

1 tablespoon (15 ml) light soy sauce

1 tablespoon (15 ml) dark soy sauce

1 teaspoon (5 ml) cornstarch (cornflour) mixed with 2 teaspoons (10 ml) water

1 tablespoon (15 ml) dark sesame oil

Rinse the wheat gluten in several changes of cold water, then cut it into round slices and set aside.

Heat a wok or large frying pan over high heat until it is hot. Add the oil, garlic, salt, and pepper. Stir-fry for 1 minute. Add the wheat gluten slices and cloud ears, and continue to stir-fry for another minute. Pour in the water, rice wine, and soy sauces, and simmer for 3 minutes. Add the cornstarch mixture and mix well. Add the sesame oil, give the mixture several good stirs, and serve at once.

FIVE-SPICE PORK RIBS

Pork spareribs are an ideal meat for this highly perfumed dish redolent of cinnamon, star anise, fennel, Sichuan peppercorns, and cloves. The result is a most poetic dish.

SERVES 4

1½ tablespoons (22 ml) peanut (groundnut) oil

1½ pounds (680 g) pork spareribs, separated and cut into 3-inch- (8-cm-) long chunks

3 cloves garlic, coarsely chopped

1 tablespoon (15 ml) five-spice powder

3 scallions (spring onions), finely chopped

2 tablespoons (30 ml) sugar

3 tablespoons (44 ml) Shaoxing rice wine or dry sherry

½ cup (4 fl oz/118 ml) Chicken Stock (page 140) or canned broth

1½ tablespoons (22 ml) light soy sauce

1 tablespoon (15 ml) dark soy sauce

Heat the wok or large frying pan until it is very hot. Add the oil and stir-fry the spareribs until they are lightly browned. Add the garlic and continue to stir-fry for 30 seconds. Add the five-spice powder, scallions, sugar, rice wine, chicken stock, and soy sauces. Turn down the heat, cover, and let simmer for 40 minutes, or until the ribs are tender.

Remove any surface fat and serve at once.

NOTE:

Have your butcher separate the spareribs into individual ribs and cut them into chunks.

Whole carved winter melon is often served at Chinese banquets, but smaller pieces can be used when it is cooked at home. The soft pulpy flesh of the melon is soothing and comforting. This soup reheats well.

SERVES 4 TO 6

- 1½ pounds (680 g) winter melon
- ¼ cup (59 ml or 2 ounces/57 g) Chinese dried mushrooms
- 4 cups (32 fl oz/992 ml) Chicken Stock (page 140) or canned broth
- ½ pound (227 g) ground pork
- ½ teaspoon (2.5 ml) salt
- 4 ounces (113 g) Virginia-style (cured) ham, shredded
- 2 scallions (spring onions), finely chopped
- 2 teaspoons (10 ml) light soy sauce

Peel the hard skin of the winter melon, scoop out the soft, pulpy interior and any seeds and discard. Cut the winter melon into 1-inch (2.5-cm) pieces. In a large pot of boiling salted water, blanch the melon pieces for 5 minutes. Drain and set aside.

Soak the mushrooms in warm water for 20 minutes. Drain them and squeeze out the excess liquid. Remove and discard the stems and cut the caps into 1-inch (2.5-cm) pieces.

In a wok or large frying pan, bring the chicken stock to a boil, then reduce the heat and simmer. Add the melon, pork, and mushrooms, and simmer for 15 minutes, or until the melon is soft. Then add the ham, scallions, and soy sauce. Simmer for another 5 minutes and serve at once.

TARO ROOT–COCONUT STEW

Taro root is a rich starch. When paired with the equally rich coconut milk and intense flavor of curry, the result is a heady vegetarian stew.

SERVES 4

- 1 tablespoon (15 ml) peanut (groundnut) oil
- 3 cloves garlic, coarsely chopped
- 1 tablespoon (15 ml) coarsely chopped ginger
- 1 pound (454 g) taro root, peeled and cut into 1-inch (2.5-cm) pieces
- 3 tablespoons (44 ml) Madras curry powder
- 1 (14-ounce/about 397-g) can coconut milk
- 3 tablespoons (44 ml) water
- 1 tablespoon (15 ml) light soy sauce
- 2 teaspoons (10 ml) chile bean sauce
- 2 teaspoons (10 ml) sugar
- 1 pound (454 g) carrots, peeled and sliced

Heat a wok or large frying pan over high heat until it is hot. Add the oil, garlic, and ginger, and stir-fry for 1 minute. Add the taro root, curry powder, coconut milk, water, soy sauce, bean sauce, and sugar. Bring the mixture to a simmer, cover, and cook for 15 minutes. Add the carrots and cook for another 15 minutes. Serve at once.

CHILE OIL OR DIPPING SAUCE

Commercial products are quite acceptable, but I include this recipe for chile oil because the homemade version really is the best. I include the spices (peppercorns and black beans) to add flavor, so I can also use it as a dipping sauce.

Makes 1 cup (237 ml)

1 cup (237 ml) peanut (groundnut) oil

1¼ cups (293 ml) coarsely chopped dried red chiles

4 tablespoons (59 ml) unroasted Sichuan
    peppercorns

3 tablespoons (44 ml) fermented black beans

Heat a wok or large frying pan over high heat and add the oil. When the oil is very hot, add the chiles, peppercorns, and beans. Turn the heat down low and stir for 1 minute. Turn off the heat and allow the mixture to cool undisturbed. Let the mixture sit 8 to 9 hours or overnight, then strain, and keep the oil in a cool, dry, dark place.

CHICKEN STOCK

Chicken stock is the foundation of Asian cooking. The usual chicken stock is precisely that: the essence of chicken, with ginger and scallion (spring onion) often added. When combined with the condiments that give Asian food its distinctive flavor, good stock captures the characteristic taste of Asia.

MAKES ABOUT 8 CUPS

4½ pounds (2 kg) uncooked chicken bones (such as bones from backs, feet, and wings)

1½ pounds (680 g) chicken parts (such as wings, thighs, and drumsticks)

9 cups (2 l) cold water

6 slices fresh ginger

9 whole scallions (spring onions)

2 teaspoons (10 ml) salt

1 teaspoon (5 ml) whole black peppercorns

Place the chicken bones and chicken pieces into a very large pot. (The bones can be used frozen or thawed.) Add the cold water to cover and bring to a simmer. Meanwhile, cut the ginger into 2 by ½- inch (5 cm by 1 cm) diagonal slices. Remove the green tops of the scallions.

Usins a large, flat spoon, skim off the scum as it rises. Regulate the heat so that the stock never boils. Keep skimming until the stock is clear, approximately 20 to 40 minutes. Do not stir the stock as it simmers.

Turn down the heat to a low simmer. Add the ginger, scallions, salt, and peppercorns. Simmer the stock on a very low heat for 2 to 4 hours, skimming any fat off the top at least twice during this time. The stock is ready when it is rich and full-bodied.

Strain the stock through several layers of dampened cheesecloth or through a very fine mesh strainer, then let it cool thoroughly. Remove any fat that has risen to the top. Use the stock within 2 days, or transfer to containers and freeze for future use.

SOOTHING CHRYSANTHEMUM–EGG FLOWER SOUP

The edible chrysanthemum was adopted centuries ago as a vegetable in China, Japan, and southeast Asia. It gives a spinachlike taste to this light soup.

SERVES 4

1 pound (454 g) fresh chrysanthemum leaves

4 cups (32 fl oz/992 ml) Chicken Stock (page 140)
   or canned broth

1 egg, lightly beaten

2 teaspoons (10 ml) dark sesame oil

1 teaspoon (5 ml) sugar

1 teaspoon (5 ml) salt

1 tablespoon (15 ml) light soy sauce

2 tomatoes, coarsely chopped

2 scallions (spring onions), finely chopped,
   white and green parts separated

Remove any tough stems from the chrysanthemum leaves and wash the leaves well. Bring a pot of water to a boil. Add the leaves and blanch for a few seconds, or until they are just wilted. Then shock them in cold water to prevent further cooking. Drain and set aside.

Put the chicken stock into a pot and bring it to a boil, then lower the heat and simmer. Meanwhile, combine the egg with the sesame oil in a small bowl. Set aside.

Add the sugar, salt, and soy sauce to the simmering stock, and stir to mix them in well. Add the tomatoes and chrysanthemum leaves and simmer for 2 minutes. Stir in the scallion whites and add the egg mixture in a very slow, thin stream. Using a chopstick or fork, pull the egg slowly into strands. (I have found that stirring the egg in a figure eight works quite well.) Garnish with the scallion tops and serve.

Index

A

Amaranth
    about, 14
    Savory Amaranth Pork
        Soup, 104
Amoy
    chile bean sauce, 55
    chile sauce, 56
    hoisin sauce, 75
    soy sauce, 98
Angles luffa. *See* Silk squash
Anise, Chinese. *See* Star anise
Anise pepper. *See* Sichuan
    peppercorns
Asparagus pea or bean. *See*
    Longbeans, Chinese
Aubergine. *See* Eggplant

B

Bamboo shoots, 15–16
Bánh tráng, 86
Barbecuing, 12
Bean curd
    about, 48–50
    fermented, 49–50
    firm, 48
    pressed seasoned, 50
    silken, 48
    soft, 48
    Stir-Fried Chinese Celery
        with Fermented Bean
        Curd, 129
Bean paste. *See* Bean sauce
Beans. *See also* Longbeans,
    Chinese
    black, 54
    Wok-Fried Fish with Black
        Bean Sauce, 108–9
Bean sauce, 50–51
Beef
    Sichuan Peppercorn Beef,
        126–27
    Stir-Fried Bitter Melon with
        Beef, 115

Bird's nest
    about, 53
    Double-Boiled Bird's Nest
        Soup, 112
Bitter melon
    about, 16–17
    Stir-Fried Bitter Melon with
        Beef, 115
Black fungus. *See* Cloud ears
Blanching, 9
Bok choy
    about, 17–18
    baby, 40
    Shanghai, 40
Braised Chicken with Tree Ears,
    120–21
Braising, 11
Broccoli, Chinese, 19
Broccoli and Citrus Peel,
    Chicken with, 110–11
Brushes, bamboo, 5

C

Cabbage, Chinese flowering,
    22–23
Cabbage, Chinese mustard, 25
Cabbage, Chinese white. *See*
    Bok choy
Cabbage, Peking, 36–37
Cabbage. preserved, 81
Carrots
    Taro Root–Coconut
        Stew, 138
Cassia, 58
Celery, Chinese
    about, 20
    Stir-Fried Chinese Celery
        with Fermented Bean
        Curd, 129
Chee Hou Sauce, 75
Chicken
    Braised Chicken with
        Tree Ears, 120–21
    Chicken Stock, 140

Chicken, *continued*
    Chicken with Broccoli and
        Citrus Peel, 110–11
    Chinese Eggplant with
        Chicken in Hoisin and
        Chile Bean Sauce, 106–7
    Double-Boiled Bird's Nest
        Soup, 112
    Lemongrass Chicken, 124
    Mu Shu–Style Chicken,
        132–33
    Spicy Shrimp-Flavored
        Chicken, 128
Chile bean paste, 55–56
Chile bean sauce
    about, 55–56
    Chinese Eggplant with
        Chicken in Hoisin and
        Chile Bean Sauce, 106–7
Chile oil
    about, 56–57
    homemade, 139
Chiles
    about, 18–19
    dried red, 57
Chinese Eggplant with Chicken
    in Hoisin and Chile Bean
    Sauce, 106–7
Chinese Pancakes, 133–34
Chinese pepper. *See* Sichuan
    peppercorns
Chives, Chinese
    about, 21
    Stir-Fried Rice Noodles
        with Yellow Chives,
        116–17
Chopping, 8
Chrysanthemum-Egg Flower
    Soup, Soothing, 141
Cilantro. *See* Coriander
Cinnamon bark, 58
Citronella grass, 34
Citrus peel
    about, 59–60
    Chicken with Broccoli and
        Citrus Peel, 110–11
    making, 60
Clay pots, 5–6
Cleavers, 5
Cloud ears
    about, 60–61
    Braised Chicken with Tree
        Ears, 120–21

Stir-Fried Vegetarian Wheat
    Gluten, 135
Coconut Stew, Taro Root–, 138
Coriander, 27
Corn oil, 61
Curry pastes and powders, 62

D
Daikon. *See* Radish,
    Chinese white
Deep-frying, 10–11
Diagonal slicing, 7
Dicing, 7
Dipping sauce, chile
    about, 56–57
    homemade, 139
Double-Boiled Bird's Nest
    Soup, 112
Doufu. See Bean curd
Duck eggs
    preserved, 66–67
    thousand-year-old, 67

E
Eggplant
    about, 28–29
    Chinese Eggplant with
        Chicken in Hoisin and
        Chile Bean Sauce, 106–7
Eggs
    duck, 66–67
    Soothing
        Chrysanthemum–Egg
        Flower Soup, 141
    Stir-Fried Shark's Fin with
        Eggs, 113
Equipment, 3–6

F
Fagara. *See* Sichuan peppercorns
Fish
    dried, 63–64
    Wok-Fried Fish with Black
        Bean Sauce, 108–9
Fish sauce, 72–73
Five-spice powder
    about, 73–74
    Five-Spice Pork Ribs, 136
Flat slicing, 7
Flying Lion Phy Quoc Fish
    Sauce, 73

G

Gaai choy. *See* Cabbage,
    Chinese mustard
Garlic
    about, 29–30
    shoots, 30–31
    Stir-Fried Water Spinach
        with Garlic, 114
Ginger
    about, 31–33
    juice, 33
    Stir-Fried Silk Squash with
        Ginger and Oyster
        Sauce, 105
Globe peanut oil, 80
Gold Blum Chinkiang
    Vinegar, 89
Golden needles. *See* Lily buds
Green onions. *See* Scallions
Guangzhou, 31

H

Hoisin sauce
    about, 74–75
    Chinese Eggplant with
        Chicken in Hoisin and
        Chile Bean Sauce, 106–7
    Hoisin-Marinated Spareribs,
        125
Hop Sing Lung Oyster Flavored
    Sauce, 78
Horizontal slicing, 7

J, K

Jicama, 33
Kale, Chinese. *See* Broccoli,
    Chinese
Kiangsi, 39
Kikkoman soy sauce, 98
Koon Chun Sauce Factory
    bean sauce, 51
    hoisin sauce, 75
    plum sauce, 80
    red rice vinegar, 89
    soy sauce, 98

L

Lan Chi
    chile bean sauce, 55
    sesame paste, 91
Leeks, Chinese, 23

Lemongrass
    about, 34
    Lemongrass Chicken, 124
Lily buds
    about, 75
    Mu Shu–Style Chicken,
        132–33
Lily stems. *See* Lily buds
Lion peanut oil, 80
Longbeans, Chinese
    about, 24
    Simple Stir-Fried Chinese
        Longbeans, 119
Lotus root, 35

M

Ma Ling hoisin sauce, 75
Mange tout. *See* Snow peas
Marinating, 8
Mincing, 8
Mooli. *See* Radish, Chinese
    white
Mu-er. See Cloud ears
Mushrooms
    Braised Chicken with Tree
        Ears, 120–21
    Chinese dried black, 76–77
    cloud ears, 60–61
    shiitake, 76
    Stir-Fried Vegetarian Wheat
        Gluten, 135
    Winter Melon Soup, 137
Mu Shu–Style Chicken, 132–33
Mustard greens, preserved, 81

N

Nam pla. See Fish sauce
Napa cabbage. *See* Cabbage,
    Peking
Noodles
    bean thread, 52
    cellophane, 52
    egg, 67–71
    rice, 85–86
    Sesame Noodles, 118
    Sha He, 85–86
    Shrimp Rolls, 130–31
    Stir-Fried Rice Noodles
        with Yellow Chives,
        116–17
    transparent, 52
    wheat, 67–71
Nuớc mắm. See Fish sauce

O

Okra, Chinese. *See* Silk squash
Orange peel, dried, 59–60
Oyster sauce
    about, 77–78
    Stir-Fried Silk Squash with
      Ginger and Oyster
      Sauce, 105

P

Pak choi. *See* Bok choy
Pancakes, Chinese, 133–34
Parsley, Chinese. *See* Coriander
Peanut oil, 79–80
Peanuts
    about, 78–79
    removing skins, 79
Pearl River Bridge
    bean sauce, 51
    black beans, 54
    hoisin sauce, 75
    sesame paste, 91
    shrimp paste, 96
    soy sauce, 98, 99
    sweet rice vinegar, 90
    white rice vinegar, 90
Peas
    shoots, 36
    snow, 42
Peas, Chinese. *See* Longbeans,
    Chinese
Peking cabbage, 36–37
Peppers. *See* Chiles
Plum sauce, 80–81
Poaching, 9
Pork
    Five-Spice Pork Ribs, 136
    Hoisin-Marinated Spareribs,
      125
    Red Pork with Chinese
      White Radish, 122–23
    Savory Amaranth Pork
      Soup, 104
    Stir-Fried Rice Noodles
      with Yellow Chives,
      116–17
    Winter Melon Soup, 137
Prawns. *See* Shrimp

R

Racks, 4–5
Radish, Chinese white
    about, 26–27
    Red Pork with Chinese
      White Radish, 122–23
Red-braising, 11
Red-in-the-snow cabbage. *See*
    Amaranth
Red Pork with Chinese White
    Radish, 122–23
Rice. *See also* Shaoxing rice
    wine
    about, 82–84
    black, 83–84
    long-grain white, 82
    noodles, 85–86
    red, 84
    short-grain white, 83
Rice papers
    about, 86–87
    Shrimp Rolls, 130–31
Rice vinegars, 88–90
Roasting, 12
Roll cutting, 7

S

Sa Cheng Oyster Flavored
    Sauce, 78
Sand pots, 5–6
Savory Amaranth Pork
    Soup, 104
Scallions, 38
Scoring, 8
Seafood
    dried, 63–64
    shark's fin, 94–95
    Shrimp Rolls, 130–31
    Stir-Fried Shark's Fin with
      Eggs, 113
    Wok-Fried Fish with Black
      Bean Sauce, 108–9
Sesame Noodles, 118
Sesame oil, 90–91
Sesame paste, 91
Sesame seeds
    about, 92
    toasting, 92
Sha He noodles, 85–86
Shallots, 39
Shallow-frying, 11
Shanghai bok choy, 40

Shaoxing rice wine, 93–94
Shark's fin
    about, 94–95
    Stir-Fried Shark's Fin
        with Eggs, 113
Shredding, 7
Shrimp
    dried, 65
    Shrimp Rolls, 130–31
Shrimp paste
    about, 96
    Spicy Shrimp-Flavored
        Chicken, 128
Shrimp roe, dried, 66
Shrimp sauce, 96
Sichuan chile sauce. See Chile
    bean sauce
Sichuan peppercorns
    about, 96–97
    Chile Oil or Dipping
        Sauce, 139
    roasting, 97
    Sichuan Peppercorn Beef,
        126–27
Silk squash
    about, 41
    Stir-Fried Silk Squash
        with Ginger and Oyster
        Sauce, 105
Simple Stir-Fried Chinese
    Longbeans, 119
Slicing, 6–7
Slow-simmering, 11
Snake bean. See Longbeans,
    Chinese
Snow peas, 42
Soothing Chrysanthemum–Egg
    Flower Soup, 141
Soups
    Double-Boiled Bird's Nest
        Soup, 112
    Savory Amaranth Pork
        Soup, 104
    Soothing
        Chrysanthemum–Egg
        Flower Soup, 141
    Winter Melon Soup, 137
Soybean condiment, 50–51
Soybeans. See Bean curd; Beans;
    Chile Bean Sauce
Soy sauces
    about, 98–99

dark, 99
light, 99
mushroom, 99
shrimp-flavored, 99
Soy Superior Sauce, 99
Spareribs, Hoisin-Marinated, 125
Spatulas, 4
Spicy Shrimp-Flavored
    Chicken, 128
Spinach, Chinese. See Amaranth
Spring onions. See Scallions
Squash. See Silk squash;
        Winter melon
Star anise, 100
Steaming, 5, 11–12
Steeping, 11
Stir-Fried Bitter Melon with
        Beef, 115
Stir-Fried Chinese Celery
        with Fermented Bean
        Curd, 129
Stir-Fried Rice Noodles with
        Yellow Chives, 116–17
Stir-Fried Shark's Fin with
        Eggs, 113
Stir-Fried Silk Squash with
        Ginger and Oyster
        Sauce, 105
Stir-Fried Vegetarian Wheat
        Gluten, 135
Stir-Fried Water Spinach with
        Garlic, 114
Stir-frying, 9–10
Stock, Chicken, 140
Sugar
    about, 100–101
    brown, 101
    malt, 101
    rock, 100
    yellow lump, 100
Sugar peas. See Snow peas

T
Tangerine peel, dried, 59–60
Taro
    about, 43
    Taro Root–Coconut Stew,
        138
Techniques
    cooking, 9–12
    cutting, 6–8
    other preparation, 8–9

Thickening, 8–9
Thousand-year-old eggs, 67
Tiger lily buds. *See* Lily buds
Tofu. *See* Bean curd
Tree ears. *See* Cloud ears
Twice-cooking, 12

V

Velveting, 9
Viet Huong Three Crab Brand
    Fish Sauce, 73
Vinegars, rice, 88–90

W

Water chestnuts, 44
Water spinach
    about, 45
    Stir-Fried Water Spinach
        with Garlic, 114

Wheat gluten
    about, 101
    Stir-Fried Vegetarian Wheat
        Gluten, 135
Wild pepper. *See* Sichuan
        peppercorns
Winter melon
    about, 46
    Winter Melon Soup, 137
Wok-Fried Fish with Black
    Bean Sauce, 108–9
Woks and wok accessories, 3–5
Wonton wrappers, 102
Wood ears or fungus. *See*
        Cloud ears

Y

Yam bean. *See* Jicama
Yang Jiang Preserved Beans
    (with Ginger), 54

Resources

Here are a selection of well-stocked Asian specialty markets.
*Offers mail-order service.

*Kam Man Food Products
200 Canal Street
New York, NY 10013
(212) 571-0330

Ming's Market
1102 Washington Street
Boston, MA 02118
(617) 338-1588

Orient Delight Market
865 East El Camino Real
Mountain View, CA 94040
(415) 969-4288

*South China Seas Trading
Company
1689 Johnston Street
Granville Island Market
Vancouver, BC V6H 3R9
(604) 681-5402

Wah Young Company
717 South King
Seattle, WA 98225
(206) 622-2416

Ken Hom's Asian Vegetables Poster

From Amaranth to Winter Melon, this high-quality art poster is an attractive and convenient display of over 30 of the most essential vegetables in East Asian cooking. With descriptions and shopping and storage tips; 24 by 36 inches, available rolled, shrink-wrapped, or laminated.

Ken Hom's Asian Ingredients Poster

More than 30 of the staples of the Asian pantry are pictured and described in this lovely, high-quality art poster—a decorative and useful addition to any kitchen wall; 24 by 36 inches, available rolled, shrink-wrapped, or laminated.

Available from your local bookstore, or order direct from the publisher. Write or call for our complete catalog of over 500 books, posters, and tapes.

TEN SPEED PRESS
P.O. Box 7123
Berkeley, CA 94707
Order phone: (800) 841-2665
fax: (510) 559-1629

ABOUT THE AUTHOR

Ken Hom is the author of eight internationally best-selling cookbooks, and has been described by Craig Claiborne of the *New York Times* as "one of the world's greatest authorities on Chinese cooking." His celebrated television series, *Ken Hom's Chinese Cookery* was shown throughout the world—on the BBC in the U.K., and on public television in America. He has recently completed the filming of his new major BBC-TV series, *Ken Hom's Hot Wok,* which will air in 1996 on the BBC in the U.K., on public television in America, and on ABC in Australia.

Ken Hom now travels the world, as a sought-after food and restaurant consultant, as a teacher and conductor of cooking demonstrations, and as a radio and television personality. In 1993, he opened his London restaurant, Imperial City, which London's *Independent* named "Chinese Restaurant of the Year," and which *Vogue* has called one of the best Chinese restaurants in Europe.

Born in America, he studied medieval art history and was formerly a professional photographer and free-lance television producer. He now lives in America and in Europe.